PYTHON PROWESS: A BEGINNER'S GUIDE

PARTHASARATHY G BALAJI G.N. KALAIVANI K
KOPPERUNDEVI N

To the Almighty God

Contents

Foreword

Welcome to the exciting world of Python programming! In this ever-evolving landscape of technology, Python stands out as a versatile and powerful language that has become the backbone of countless applications, from web development and data science to artificial intelligence and automation.

As technology continues to shape our daily lives, the ability to code has become an invaluable skill. Python, with its simplicity, readability, and extensive libraries, has emerged as the language of choice for both beginners and seasoned developers alike. This book serves as your gateway into the Python universe, offering a comprehensive and hands-on approach to mastering this programming language.

Whether you are a student embarking on your programming journey, a professional looking to enhance your skill set, or an enthusiast eager to explore the endless possibilities of coding, this book is crafted with you in mind. The journey through these pages will not only equip you with the fundamentals of Python but also empower you to tackle real-world challenges with confidence.

As you delve into the intricacies of Python, you will discover its elegance and flexibility. Python's readability encourages clean and maintainable code, while its extensive standard library and vibrant community ensure that you have the tools and support needed to bring your ideas to life. The beauty of Python lies not only in its simplicity but also in its scalability – from small scripts to large-scale applications, Python is adaptable to your needs.

So, let the adventure begin! Immerse yourself in the world of Python, embrace the challenges, celebrate the victories, and, most importantly, enjoy the process of becoming a proficient Python programmer. May this book be your trusted companion on this exciting voyage into the heart of programming.

Preface

The book " **Python Prowess**" has been prepared to meet the requirement of people who are willing to learn basic programming skills using python. The python programming has been covered fully describing the subject matter in a simple language. A large number of programs have been added wherever required. This book divided into six chapters:

Chapter 1: Introduction

Chapter 2: Conditional and Control Statements

Chapter 3: Lists,Tuples and Dictionaries

Chapter 4: Strings and Functions

Chapter 5: File Handling

Chapter 6: Practice Programs

Each chapter contains a number of example programs to explain the techniques to solve a problem. All efforts have been made to keep errors to barest minimum. However, there is a possibility that some errors might have crept in inadvertently. We, would, therefore be grateful is such oversights are pointed out by the readers. Suggestions for improvement of the text from readers are welcome.

-Authors

Acknowledgements

First of all, we may acknowledge the almighty god's choices and abundant blessings.

We express my sincere gratitude to my esteemed founder chancellor, **Dr. G. Viswanathan**, for his sincere endeavor in educating us in this premier institution. At this pleasing moment of having successfully completed our book, We wish to our sincere thanks and gratitude to our institution **Vellore Institute of Technology**, **Vellore** for providng all the facilities.

Prologue

Welcome to the exciting world of Python programming! Whether you're a curious beginner or an enthusiastic learner, this book is your passport to unlocking the mysteries of coding and harnessing the power of Python. Prepare to embark on a journey that will demystify programming concepts, empower you with practical skills, and instill a love for the art of coding.

Chapter 1: Introduction

In this inaugural chapter, we'll set the stage for your Python adventure. From understanding the basics of programming to exploring the philosophy behind Python's design, you'll gain insights that will pave the way for a solid foundation. Get ready to dive into the world of code with confidence and a clear understanding of what lies ahead.

Chapter 2: Conditional and Control Statements

Now that you've got your feet wet, let's take the plunge into the fundamental building blocks of programming. Chapter 2 delves into conditional statements and control structures, teaching you how to make decisions in your code and control the flow of execution. Brace yourself for a hands-on experience that will sharpen your logical thinking and problem-solving skills.

Chapter 3: Lists, Tuples, and Dictionaries

Arrays, tuples, and dictionaries, oh my! Chapter 3 introduces you to essential data structures in Python. You'll learn how to organize and manipulate data efficiently, paving the way for more sophisticated programs. With a solid grasp of these structures, you'll be equipped to tackle a variety of real-world coding challenges.

Chapter 4: Strings and Functions

Strings are not just a sequence of characters; they're the threads that weave your code together. Chapter 4 dives into the world of strings and functions, teaching you how to manipulate text and create reusable code blocks. By the end of this chapter, you'll be crafting elegant functions and transforming data with ease.

Chapter 5: File Handling

In the digital landscape, files are your gateways to persistence. Chapter 5 explores the art of file handling in Python, showing you how to read and write data to external files. Uncover the secrets of data persistence and broaden your programming horizons as you interact with the wider world of information storage.

Chapter 6: Practice Programs

Theory without practice is like a ship without a sea. In Chapter 6, you'll put your newfound knowledge to the test with a series of engaging practice programs. These exercises are designed to reinforce your skills, challenge your problem-solving abilities, and solidify your understanding of Python programming.

Are you ready to embark on this coding journey? Let's turn the page and delve into the fascinating world of Python!

## CHAPTER ONE

Introduction

In the real world, any business need solutions using automation, and the developer must have them, to rise to more challenging and lucrative software development and engineering positions. The programming language that expands the most entries is Python. If a programmer has a solid grasp of Python, they can work in many different industries and roles.

Guido van Rossum released the first version of Python On February 20, 1991. The Python programming language takes its title from the Monty Python's Flying Circus television humor sequence, even if many of us may only think of the python as a vast serpent.

Learning Python takes a lesser amount time than learning many other languages, making it probable to begin programming more rapidly. It is simple to use for creating new software, and with Python, it is normally probable to make code more quickly. Python is free ,open source platform and simple to get, mount, and install.

1.1 Python Advantages

In 1999, Guido van Rossum outlined his objectives for Python. It is simple syntax language that is powerful as those of the major rivals. This open-source package allowing everyone to contribute to its expansion. Python code that is as easy to understand as plain English suitable for routine tasks, allowing for rapid development times.

Python is a fantastic programming language to learn. There are several causes behind this, but the most straightforward one is that it's quick and simple to create; it doesn't take long to come up with functional code that accomplishes anything important. Python's extremely user-friendly syntax makes it simple to create elegant programs. The core language is quite easy to learn and retain, and it also contains a large library of built-in functions that you may utilize to speed up the majority of routine computer activities.

Python software is available for a variety of operating systems, including Windows, Linux and Mac, This also supports various operating systems, including IBM i, AIX, and Solaris. The examples in this book are presented using the most recent version of Python, 3.11. Like other programming languages, there are various building blocks available to construct the code for real life problems. The explanation of each block will be discussed in forthcoming sections.

1.2 Data types

Variable types are specified using Python Data Types. It specifies the kind of data that will be kept in a variable. Many different categories of data can be saved in memory. For instance, a person's name is kept as a sequence of alphabetic letters, and their age is stored as a numeric value. Python has various built-in data types which will be described below.

Numeric: int, float, complex

String: str

Sequence : list, tuple, range

Binary : bytes, byte array, memory view

Mapping : dict

Boolean : bool

Set : set, frozen set

None – None Type

1.3 Variables

Assume a variable as a name given to a specific object. Variables do not need to be declared or defined earlier in Python, unlike many other programming languages. You can create a variable by simply giving it a value before using it. A single equals symbol (=) is used for assignment.

Example:

a=10

1.4 Expression

In Python, identifiers, operators, and operands are found as expressions. A class, variable, or function are defined and known by a name called an identifier. An operand is a thing that is being worked on. An operator, on the other hand, is a unique symbol that carries out the arithmetic or logical operations on the operands. Python has a wide variety of operators and discussed in Section 1.6.

1.5 Statements

An instruction that a Python interpreter can carry out is called a statement. Therefore, anything written in Python is a statement, to put it simply. A statement in Python terminates with the token character NEWLINE. It recommends that a Python script has statements on each line.

In Python, statements can drop into one of four types: print, assignment, conditional and looping statements. The assignment and print statements are frequently employed in most of the programs. A value is the output of a print statement. The only thing that an assignment statement does is allocate a value to the operand on its left side.

Conditional statements is the order in which statements or blocks of code are executed at runtime based on a condition. The loop allows us to repeatedly go through each item in the sequence and do the same set of actions on each one. Users can efficiently automate and repeat processes using Python's loop statements.

1.6 Operators

Operators are special symbols that execute operations on variables and values. The various types of operators are given below.

1.6.1 Arithmetic operators

Operator	Name	Example
+	Addition	24 + 4 = 28
-	Subtraction	24 – 4 = 20
*	Multiplication	10 * 4 = 40
/	Division	10 / 4 = 10
//	Floor Division	10 // 3 = 3
%	Modulo	10 % 3 = 1
**	Power	5 ** 3 = 125

1.6.2 Assignment Operators

Operator	Name	Example
=	Assignment	x = 7
+=	Addition Assignment	x += 1 or x = x + 1
-=	Subtraction Assignment	x -= 3 or x = x - 3
*=	Multiplication Assignment	x *= 4 or x = x * 4
/=	Division Assignment	x /= 3 or x = x / 3
%=	Remainder Assignment	x %= 10 or x = x % 10
**=	Exponent Assignment	x **= 10 or x = x ** 10

1.6.3 Comparison Operators

Operator	Name	Example
==	Is Equal To	7 == 7 is True
!=	Not Equal To	2 != 5 is True
>	Greater Than	4 > 5 is False
<	Less Than	4 < 5 is True
>=	Greater Than or Equal To	3 >= 5 is False
<=	Less Than or Equal To	3 <= 5 is True

1.6.4 Logical Operators

Operator	Name	Example
and	x and y	Logical AND
or	x or y	Logical OR
not	not x	Logical NOT

1.6.5 Bitwise Operators

Operator	Name	Example
&	Bitwise AND	x & y
|	Bitwise OR	x | y
~	Bitwise NOT	~x
^	Bitwise XOR	x ^ y
>>	Bitwise right shift	x >> 2 (2 indicates number of bits to be shifted right side)
<<	Bitwise left shift	x << 2 (2 indicates number of bits to be shifted left side)

1.6.6 Special Operators

(i) Identity operators

In Python, *is* and *is not* are used to check if two values are situated on the same portion of the memory. Two variables that are equal does not imply that they are identical.

Operators:- is, is not,

(ii) Membership operators

In Python, *in and not in* are the membership operators. They are used to check whether a value or variable is found in a sequence (string, list, tuple, set and dictionary).

Operators: in , not in

(iii) Indentation

Indentation mentions to the spaces at the beginning of a code line. In other programming languages the indentation in code is for readability only, in Python is very important. Python uses indentation to specify a block of code.

Example
if 7>5:
print("Seven is greater than two")

(iv) Comments

In python programming, if you want comment the particular line,# symbol is used. The particular line is ignored while executing the code.

# This is a python programming
print("Hello, World!")

Since Python will ignore string literals that are not assigned to a variable, user can add a multiline string in implementation, and place your comment inside it:

```
"""
This is a comment
in python programming
to ignore the multiple lines.
"""
```

The solution is to be provided for problems using logical constructs like Algorithm, Flow chart and Pseudo Code.

1.7 . Algorithm

A set of instructions called an algorithm is a precise computing procedure that accepts an input value or set of values, process it and display the output value. To put it another way, an algorithm is a process that collects data and uses it to alter it according to predetermined stages, eventually filling the required unknown with the desired value.

1.7.1 Advantages Algorithm

- Less time is enough
- Requires small amount of memory.
- The successful or appropriate solution.
- All instructions must be followed in the proper order, and some may be repeated several times or until a specific requirement is satisfied.
- Algorithms are frequently built to handle a variety of input data when solving a single problem.

Example:
Problem: Algorithm for addition of any two numbers.
Step 1: START
Step 2: READ a,b
Step 3: CALCULATE c=a+b
Step 4: DISPLAY c
Step 5:STOP
To understand the problem statement, flow chart plays an important role.

1.8 Flow Chart

A diagram that depicts a workflow or process is called a flowchart. Another definition of a flowchart is a diagrammatic explanation of an algorithm or a step-by-step process for solving a problem.

1.8.1 Symbols used in Flow Chart

The following symbols are used to draw flow chart for the given problem.

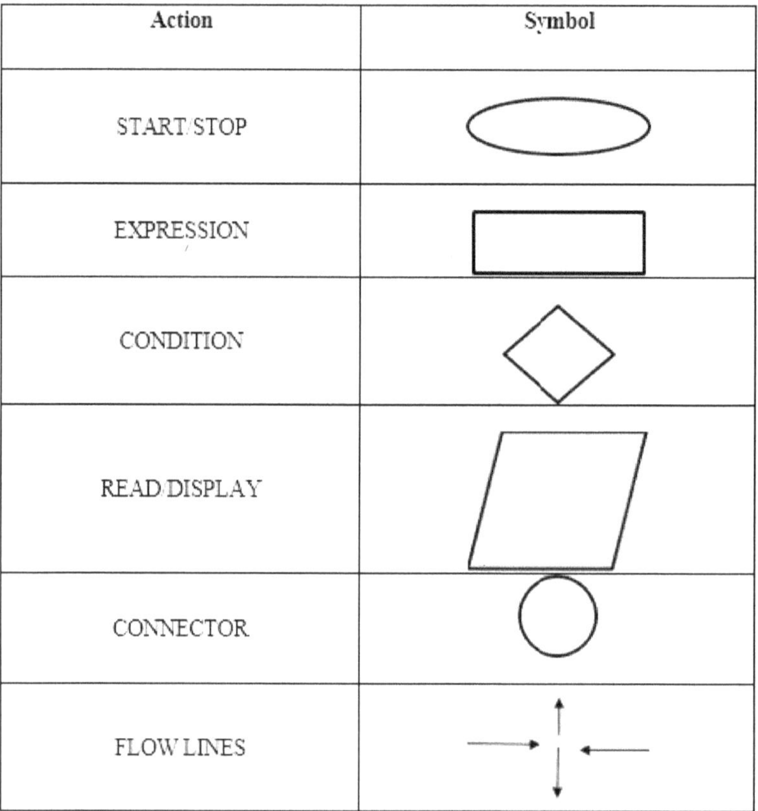

Action	Symbol
START/STOP	
EXPRESSION	
CONDITION	
READ/DISPLAY	
CONNECTOR	
FLOW LINES	

Figure 1.1 List of symbols used in Flow chart

1.8.2 Advantages of Flow Chart

- Easy to make for the problem
- Communication becomes effective and easy to know
- Mistakes can be easily identified
- Analysis becomes effective
- Synthesis becomes effective
- Debugging becomes possible
- Logics can be easily construed.

1.9. Pseudo Code

Pseudo code is a *false or imitation code*. It is also called as Program Design Language (PDL). A clear understandable explanation of what an algorithm or computer program should perform is known as pseudocode. It is written in a intelligible manner with normal grammar and syntax so that systems analyst and other people contributing in the development process may easily understand it.

1.9.1 Guideline for Pseudocode

a. Write one statement per line

Each statement in pseudo code represents a single action and is written on a separate line.

b. Capitalize keywords

The keywords should be written in capital letters

c. Indent to show hierarchy

Indentation is a process of showing the boundaries of the structure

d. End multiline structure

Each structure must be ended properly which provides more clarity.

e. Keep statement language independent

Programming languages have special capabilities that are note available in other languages
Example
Pseudo code for multiplying two numbers
START
READ a,b
c=a*b
PRINT c
STOP

1.10 Mode of Execution

Python executes source code using an interpreter. There are two different available to use the interpreter in python.

(i) Interactive Mode

A single statement can be executed at a time in this mode. Additionally, users must type the statement in front of the '>>>' and click enter to use the interactive mode. This quickly produces the output of that specific statement. To view the immediate output, this mode is simple and practical to use. However, users are also unable to save the entire program and must repeatedly write it in order to run it.
Example: Interactive mode in Python

```
Python 3.10.7 (tags/v3.10.7:6cc6b13, Sep  5 2022, 14:08:36) [MSC v.1933 64 bit (
AMD64)] on win32
Type "help", "copyright", "credits" or "license()" for more information.
>>> print("welcome to python")
welcome to python
>>> a=int(input())
5
>>> print(a)
5
>>>
```

Figure 2. Interactive mode

ii.

Script Mode in Python

In script mode, the entire source code must be written and saved as a Python source code file. Uses save the source code with the extension of ".py".

Example.py

```
a=int(input("enter first number"))
b=int(input("enter second number"))
c=a*b
print("the answer is",c)
```

Figure 3. Script mode

Summary

- Real world problem solving is done by algorithm,flowchart,pseduo code and program

- Python consists of various programming elements data type, constants, variables and operators.
- Python programs can be exectued by interactive mode and script mode.

Sample Programs

 # Program to print the area of circle

```
r=float(input("Enter radius:"))
area=(22/7)*r*r
print("Area is",area)
```

Output:

```
Enter radius:34
Area is 3633.1428571428573
```

#Program 2

 # Program to print the area of rectangle

```
l=float(input("Enter length:-"))
b=float(input("Enter breadth:-"))
area=l*b
print("Area is",area)
```

Output:

```
Enter length:-6
Enter breadth:-7
Area is 42.0
```

Conditional Statements

Generally, an algorithm is representing a process in sequence as a solution to any problem statement. The steps involved in solving those steps are statements, selection of variables, flow of control and functioning of selected variables. Here, flow of control is processed using control flow logic. Control flow refers to the order in which program statements are executed, i.e., when the execution of one statement is complete, the computer control passes to the next statement in the code. This process is similar to reading the text, figures and tables on a page of a book. In programs instructions are executed sequentially one by one in the order in which they come into sight in the program. Of course, this is a fundamental programming concept for beginners to develop simple programs. It is not advisable to have a sequential program writing style for solving every problem.

Quite often, it is advantageous in a program to alter the sequence of the flow of statements depending upon the circumstances. In real-time applications, there are a number of situations where a programmer has to change the order of execution of statements based on certain conditions. Therefore, when a programmer desires the control flow to be non-sequential then he/she may use control structures or decision statements. Thus, decision making statements help a programmer in transferring the control from one statement to another in the program. In short, a programmer decides which statement is to be executed based on a condition.

2.1 DECISION MAKING STATEMENTS

Python language supports various decision-making statements, they are:

- if statements
- if-else statements
- Nested if statements
- if-elif-else statements

2.1.1 if Statement

The **"if"** keyword used in program executes a statement only if a given condition is true. The syntax for if statement is shown in Figure 2.1.

$$if\ condition:$$

$$statement(s)$$

Figure 2.1. Syntax for **"if"** statement

The keyword if begins the if statement. The condition is a Boolean expression which determines whether or not the body of if block will be executed. A colon (:) must always be followed by the condition. The block may contain one or more statements. The statement or statements are executed if and only if the condition within the if statement is true. The algorithm and flow chart for if statement is given in Figure 2.2.

Algorithm:

Step1: Initialization.

Step 2: Checking with conditional statement with "if" keyword.

Step3: If the condition is true, execute the statements under the if statements

Step 4: if the condition is false exit the "if" block

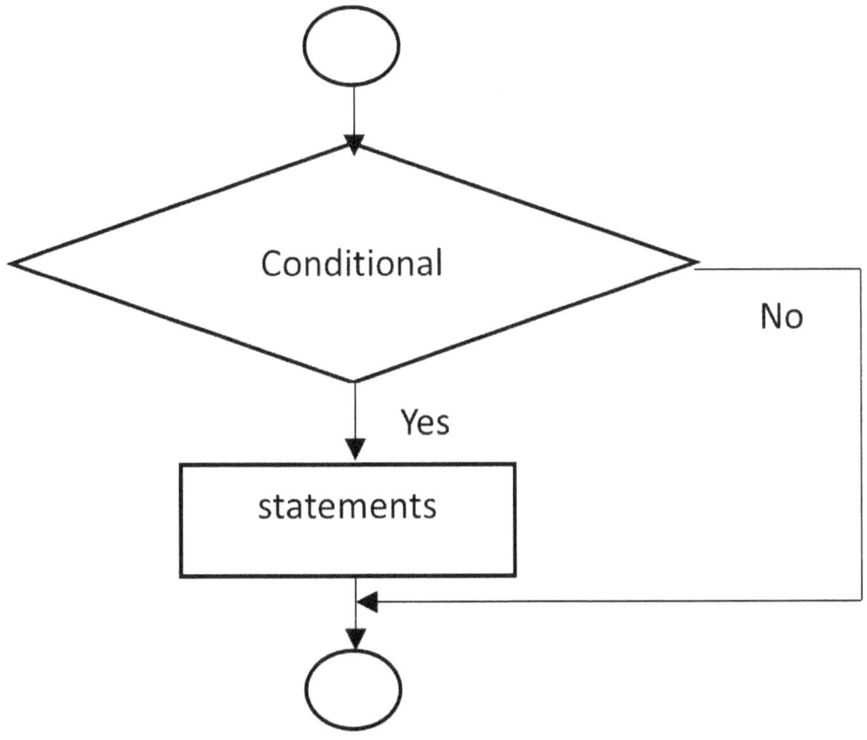

Figure 2.2: "if" - Algorithm and Flow Chart

<u>Sample program: Print Whether the Given Number is Even Number</u>
num=eval(input("Enter the number: "))
if num%2==0:
print("The number is even")
<u>Output</u>
Enter the number: 16
The number is even
In the above program, a number is provided by a user. The statement within the if block is executed if and only if the number is divisible by 2 hence evaluates to True.

2.1.2 if-else Statement

The execution of the **"if"** statement has been explained in the previous section. The **"if"** statement executes when the condition is true and it does nothing when the condition is false. To address the possibility of the condition **"if-else"** statement is used. The **"if-else"** statement takes care of both true as well as a false condition. The algorithm for **"if-else"** statement is given below in Figure 2.3.

if condition:

    statement(s)

Figure 2.3. Syntax for **"if-else"** statement

The **"if-else"** statement checks both true and false conditions using two blocks. One block is for **"if"** and it may contain one or more statements, which is/are executed under true condition. The other block is for **"else"**, it may also have one or more statements which is/are executed under false condition. A colon (:) must always be followed by the condition in **"if "**line and after the keyword **"else"**. The flow chart for if-else statement is given in Figure 2.4.

<u>Algorithm:</u>

Step1: Initialization.

Step 2: Checking with conditional statement with "if" keyword.

Step3: If the condition is true, execute the statements under the *"if"* statements

Step 4: If the condition is false execute the statements under the *"else"* statements

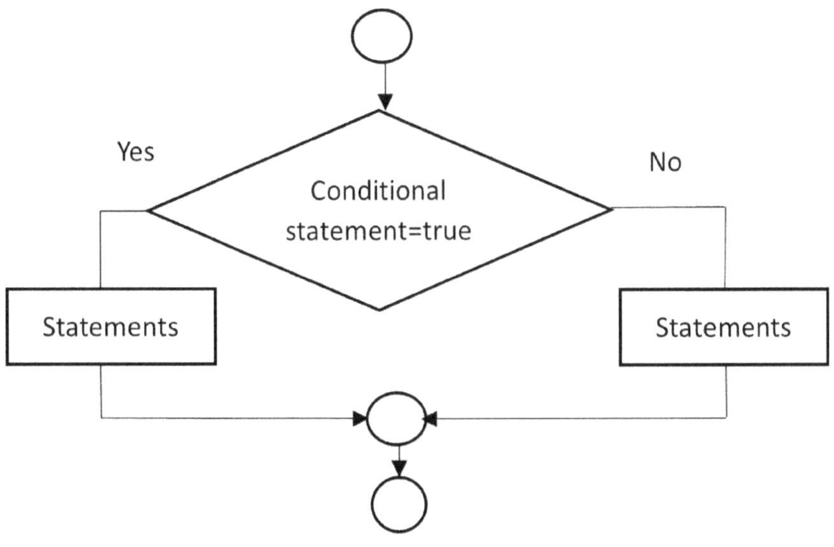

Figure 2.4. Flowchart for **"if-else"** statement

<u>Sample program: To Print greatest of two numbers entered by the user</u>
num_1=int(input("Enter the First Number:"))
num_2=int(input("Enter the Second Number:"))
if num_1>num_2:
print("Greatest number is:",num_1)
else:
print("Greatest number is:",num_2)
<u>Output:</u>
Enter the First Number:50
Enter the Second Number:24
Greatest number is: 50
In the above program, two numbers are provided by user. When the condition is true, if block is executed, for false condition else block is executed.

2.1.3 Nested if Statements

When **"if"** function is called within other **"if"** function then the statements are known as **nested if** statements.

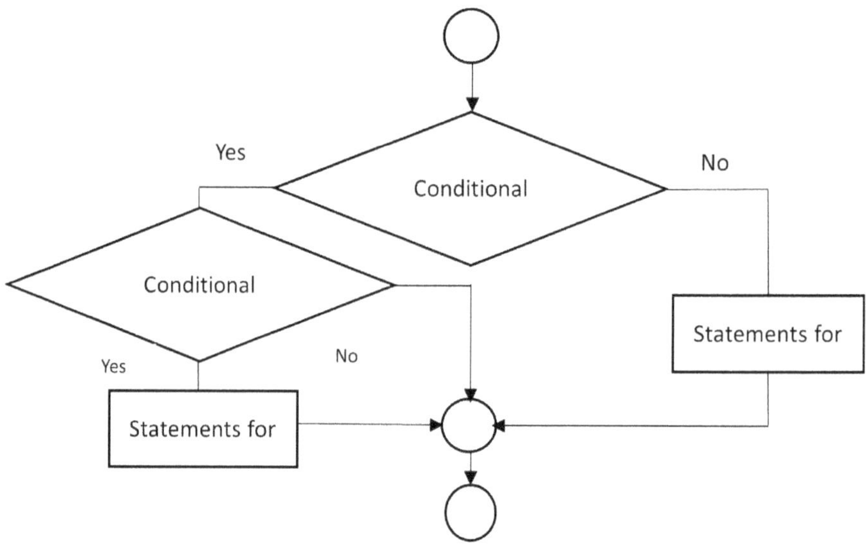

Figure 2.5. Nested **"if"** statement

Figure 2.6. Flowchart of Nested if statement

Sample program: To Print highest score of a student in his examination (min of three subjects)

```
mark1=int(input("Enter the mark of first subject:"))
mark2=int(input("Enter the mark of second subject:"))
mark3=int(input("Enter the mark of third subject:"))
if mark1>mark2:
if mark1>mark3:
print(mark1,"is greater than ",mark2,"and ",mark3)
else:
```

```
print(mark1,"is lesser than ",mark2,"and ",mark3)
```
Output

Enter the mark of first subject:74

Enter the mark of second subject:58

Enter the mark of third subject:63

74 is greater than 58 and 63

In the above program, three marks are provided

2.1.4 if-elif-else Statements

In **"if-elif-else"** statements the **"if"** statement executes when the condition is true, for the false condition, it checks with **"elif"** condition and executes the statements under it. Even though the condition is false, finally the **"else"** statements are executed. The syntax for **"if-elif-else"** statement is given in Figure 2.7.

```
if condition:

    statement(s)

elif condition:
```

Figure 2.7. Syntax for **"if-elif-else"** statement

Sample program: To Print grade of the student based on the aggregate obtained

```
mark1=input("Enter first mark")
mark2=input("Enter second mark")
mark3=input("Enter third mark")
mark4=input("Enter fourth mark")
mark5=input("Enter fifth mark")
Total = mark1+mark2+mark3+mark4+mark5
Agg= Total/5
if(Agg>=90):
print("Grade A")
```

```
elif(Agg>=70 and Agg<90)
print("Grade B")
elif(Agg>=50 and Agg<70)
print("Grade C")
else:
print("FAIL")
```

2.2 Loop Statements

In our daily routine certain tasks are performed repeatedly. It can be tedious to perform such tasks using pen and paper. For instance, teaching a concept to multiple classes of students can become easier if the teacher uses a simple computer program with loop instructions instead of pen and paper. This can be done more easily using loop in Python. Loops are used to repeat the same code multiple times. Python provides two types of loop statements the while and for loops. The while loop is controlled by a condition, whether the given condition is true or false, hence it is condition-controlled loop. The for loop is a count-controlled loop which repeats for a specific number of times.

2.2.1 while Loop

The while loop is a loop control statement in Python and frequently used in programming for repeated execution of statement(s) in a loop. It executes a sequence of statements repeatedly as long as a condition remains true.

The reserved keyword **"while"** begins with the while statement. The test condition is a Boolean expression. The colon (:) must follow the test condition, i.e., the while statement be terminated with a colon (:). The statement(s) within the while loop will be executed till the condition is true, i.e., the condition is evaluated and if the condition is true then the body of the loop is executed. When the 126 Problem Solving and Python Programming condition is false, the execution will be completed out of the loop or in other words, the control goes out of the loop. The syntax for while loop is given as follows:

while condition:

   statement(s)

Figure 2.8 Syntax for **"while"** statement

Algorithm:

Step1: Initialization.

Step 2: Checking with conditional statement with "while" keyword.

Step3: If the condition is true, execute the statements under the while loop

Step 4: if the condition is false exit the loop

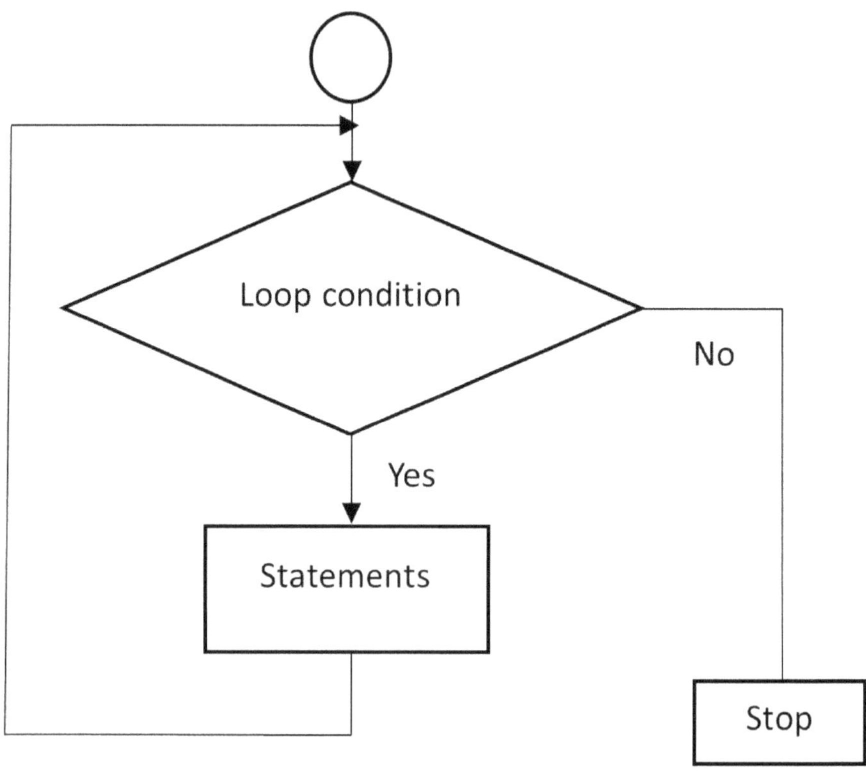

Figure 2.9 Algorithm and Flowchart for **"while"** statement

<u>Sample program:</u> Write a program to print the numbers from one to five using the while loop.

count=0 #initialize the counter

while count<=5: # Test condition

print("Count = ",count) # print the value of count count=count+1 # Increment the value of count by 1

Output

Count = 0

Count = 1

Count = 2

Count = 3

Count = 4

Count = 5

In the above program, the variable count is initialized to 0. The condition is checked with while statement whether less than or equal to 5 (count<=5), if true the print statement is executed, then the count is incremented once, again the condition is checked . It repeatedly executes the statements within the loop until count<=5. The loop terminates when the value of count reaches 6.

2.2.2 range Function

The range () is an inbuilt function in Python, which is used to generate a list of integers. The range function has one, two or three parameters. The last two parameters in range () are optional. The syntax of the range function is:
range(begin, end, step)

- The 'begin' is the first beginning number in the sequence at which the list starts.
- The 'end' is the limit, i.e., the last number in the sequence.
- The 'step' is the difference between each number in the sequence.

Sample Program:
Create a list of integers from 1 to 5.
list(range(1,20,2))
Output
[1, 3, 5, 7, 9, 11, 13, 15, 17, 19]
The range(1,20,2) function is used in the above example. It generates a list of integers starting from 1 with a difference of two between two successive integers up to 20.

TABLE 2.1 Different usability of range function

range(5)	[0,1,2,3,4]
range(1,5)	[1,2,3,4]
range(1,2,5)	[1,3]
range(5,0,-1)	[5, 4, 3, 2, 1]
range(-4,4)	[-4, -3, -2, -1, 0, 1, 2, 3]
range(0,1)	[0]
range(1,1)/ range(0)	empty

2.2.3 *for Loop*

The for loops in Python are slightly different from the for loops in other programming languages. The Python for loop iterates through a sequence of objects, i.e., it iterates through each value in a sequence, where the sequence of object holds multiple items of data stored one after another. In the forthcoming chapters, we will study various sequence type objects of Python, such as string, list and tuples. The syntax of for loop is given as follows.

for variable in sequence(variable):

statement(s)

Figure 2.10 Syntax "for" loop

The for loop is a Python statement which repeats a group of statements for a specified number of times. As described in the syntax, the keywords **"for"** and in are essential keywords to iterate the sequence of values.

Sample Program: To Print first 5 natural numbers using for loop

```
for i in range(1,6):
print(i)
print("Loop Terminated")
Output
1
2
3
4
5
Loop Terminated
```

The sequence of natural numbers from 1 to 5 is printed using for and range() function. This allows the for loop to assign the values 1, 2, 3, 4 and 5 to the iteration variable i.

2.2.4 Nested Loop

As **"if"** and **"elif"** statements the **"for"** and **"while"** loop statements can be nested in the same manner. When one loop is inserted completely within another loop, then it is called nested loop.

Sample Program: To display the pattern of numbers

1
1 2
1 2 3
1 2 3 4
1 2 3 4 5

Code:

```
num=1
x=num
for i in range(1,6,1):
num=num+1;
for j in range(1,num,1):
print(j, end=" ")
x=num+1
print()
```

2.3 "break" Statement

The keyword **break** allows a programmer to terminate a loop. When the **break** statement is encountered inside a loop, the loop is immediately terminated and the first statement following the loop is executed.

loop sequence:

    body of loop

    if condition:

        break

Figure 2.11 Syntax- break statement

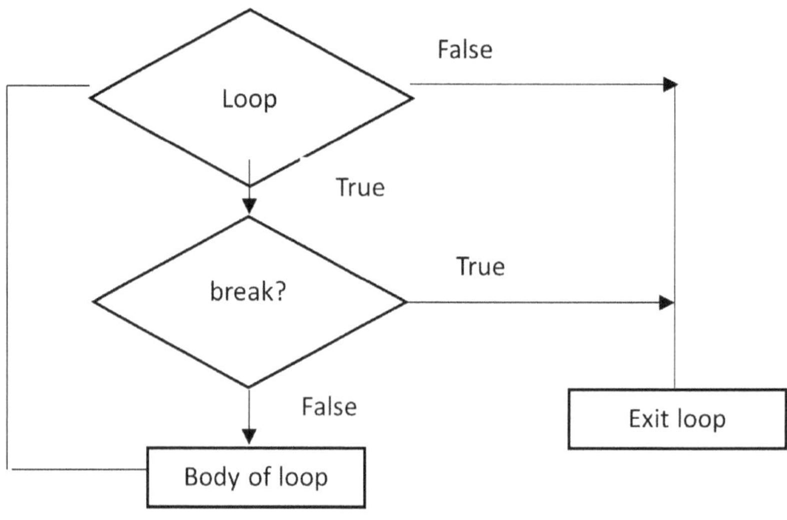

Figure: 2.12 Flowchart- break statement

<u>Sample program:</u> To display numbers
for i in range(1,11,1):
if(i%3==0:
break
else:
print(i, end=" ")
Output:
1 2
The sequence has printed 1 and 2 once the input number is divisible by 3 the loop is terminated.

2.4 continue Statement

The **"continue"** statement is used where the remaining statements within the body are skipped but the loop condition is checked to see if the loop should continue or exit. It behaves opposite to **"break"** statement.

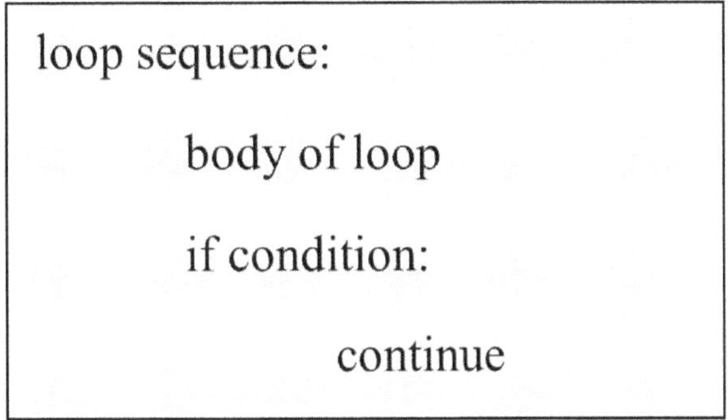

Figure 2.13 Syntax- continue statement

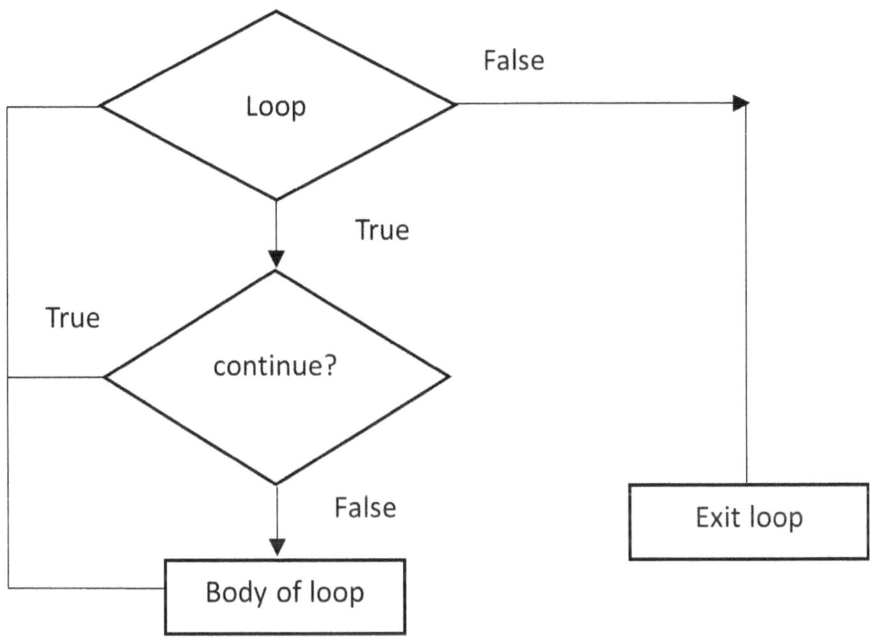

Figure 2.14 Flowchart- continue statement

Sample Program: To display numbers

for i in range(1,11,1):

```python
if(i%3==0):
continue
else:
print(i, end=" ")
```
Output:
1 2 4 5 7 8 10

The sequence has printed numbers from 1 to 10, skipping the numbers divisible by 3.

Summary

- A Boolean expression is either True and False, used a bool in python.
- Python Supports various decision statements, such as if, if-else and multi-way if-elif-else statements.
- Loop is used to execute a set of statements for fixed number of times preventing redundant statements
- Python supports two control loop statements, i.e., for loop and while loop.
- The break and continue are keywords used in loops.

#PROGRAM 1: To Find the given year is a leap year
```python
year=int(input("Enter the year"))
if(year%4 ==0):
print("Leap year")
else:
print(" Not Leap year")
```
OUTPUT:
Enter the year: 1996
Leap year
#PROGRAM 2:
Generate an electricity bill for the following information. Calculate the total amount.

Units: Cost in Rupees
<100 1
>=100 and <300 2

```
>=300 4
unit=int(input("Enter the unit value"))
if(unit<100):
Bill= unit*1
elif(unit>100 and unit<300):
Bill= unit*2
elif(unit>300):
Bill= unit*3.5
else:
print("Wrong unit")
print("Bill amount is Rs:", Bill)
```

Output:

```
Enter the unit value: 256
Bill amount is Rs:512
```

#PROGRAM 3: To Find the given number is positive or not

```
number=input("Enter the number")
if(n>0):
print("Positive number")
elif(n<0):
print("Negative number")
else:
print("Number is ZERO")
```

OUTPUT:

```
Enter the number: -64
```

Negative number

#Program 4: To print number series from 1 to 5.

```
i=1
while(i<=5):
print(i)
i=i+1
```

OUTPUT:

1

2

3

4

5

#Program 5: To print number series from 5 to 1.

```
i=5
```

```
while(i<=1):
print(i)
i=i-1
```

OUTPUT:

5

4

3

2

1

#Program 6: To find the sum of digits.

```
i=5
while(i<=1):
print(i)
i=i-1
```

OUTPUT:

5

4

3

2

1

#Program 7: To print the reverse of a given number

```
num=int(input("Enter the number to reverse:-"))
temp=0
while(num>0):
r=num%10
temp=temp*10+r
num=int(num/10)
print(temp)
```

OUTPUT:

Enter the number to reverse:- 236

632

#Program 8: To check whether the given number is palindrome or not

```
num=int(input("Enter a number to check whether palindrome:-"))
num_1=num
temp=0
while(num>0):
r=num%10
temp=temp*10+r
```

```
num=int(num/10)
if(temp==num_1):
print(num_1,"is a Palindrome")
else:
print(num_1,"is not a Palindrome")
```

OUTPUT:

Enter a number to check whether palindrome:-12

12 is not a Palindrome

Enter a number to check whether palindrome:-323

323 is a Palindrome

#Program 9: To check whether the given number is an Armstrong number

```
num=int(input("Enter a number to check if it is Armstrong number:-"))
num_1=num
temp=0
while(num>0):
r=int(num%10)
temp=temp+r*r*r
num=int(num/10)
if(temp==num_1):
print(num_1,"is an Armstrong number")
else:
print(num_1,"is not an Armstrong number")
```

OUTPUT:

Enter a number to check if it is Armstrong number:-153

153 is an Armstrong number

Enter a number to check if it is Armstrong number:-121

121 is not an Armstrong number

#Program 10: To swap two given numbers

```
num1=int(input("Enter the first number:-"))
num2=int(input("Enter the second number:-"))
temp=num1
num1=num2
num2=temp
print("After swapping the first number is:-",num1)
print("After swapping the second number is:-",num2)
```

OUTPUT:

Enter the first number:-21

Enter the second number:-35
After swapping the first number is:- 35
After swapping the second number is:-21

## CHAPTER THREE

Lists, Tuples and Dictionaries

3.1 List

Python's list is a versatile, powerful, and widely used built-in data type.The mutable sequences of objects can be created in variable-length and also we can combine objects of different types within the same list. Some Key Features of list objects:

- Ordered: The elements of the list are ordered sequentially as per the insertion order.
- Heterogeneous: List can contain different types of objects.
- Zero-based: we can access the elements of lists using indices that start at zero.
- Mutable: It is possible to change the elements
- Growable and dynamic: Size of the List can be grown and shrunk during the addition, insertion, and removal of items.
- Nestable: lists of lists can be made.
- Iterable: We can traverse the lists using a loop or comprehension.
- Sliceable: A number of elements can be taken out of them.
- Combinable: we can combine two or more lists using the concatenation operators.
- Copyable: we can make copies of the list
- using various methods.

3.1.1 Creating or Constructing Lists in Python

There are three methods to create a List by using,

- List literals
- List Constructors
- List Comprehension

(i) List literals

In Python, a list literal is a concise way to create a list. It provides a convenient syntax for initializing lists with a sequence of elements. List literals are enclosed in square brackets [], and the elements are separated by commas.

```
python
Examples:
numbers = [2,3,5,6,7,9]
months = ["January", "February", "March", "April", "May"]
matrix = [
[2, 4, 6],
[3, 6, 9],
[4, 8, 12]
]
Books = [
{"Bname": "Python", "price": 1800, "quantity": 5},
{"Bname": "C++", "price": 1200, "quantity": 4},
{"Bname": "Java", "price": 900, "quantity": 3}
]
empty = []
```

This simple syntax makes it easy to define and work with lists in a readable and expressive manner. The list can hold elements of different data types, including an integer, Boolean, string, tuple, dictionary, and another list. An empty list serves as a starting point, allowing elements to be added dynamically as needed during program execution.

```
Example:
L1= [90, "Mark", True, {"Employee": "Krishna"}, (10, 20, 30), [6.34, 7.98]]
```

(ii) list() Constructor

In Python, the list() constructor is a built-in function that allows you to create a new list. It can be used in several ways to initialize lists, convert other iterable objects to lists, or create a shallow copy of an existing list. Let's explore the various ways the list() constructor can be employed.

The list() constructor can convert other iterable objects like strings, tuples, sets, or even ranges into lists:

Syntax:

list([iterable])

Example:

string_as_list = list("hello") # Output: ['h', 'e', 'l', 'l', 'o']

tuple_as_list = list((1, 2, 3)) # Output: [1, 2, 3]

set_as_list = list({4, 5, 6}) # Output: [4, 5, 6]

range_as_list = list(range(3)) # Output: [0, 1, 2]

The list() constructor can be used to create a shallow copy of an existing list. This is useful when you want to duplicate a list without modifying the original:

In certain instances, it is acceptable to use tuples, dictionaries, strings, and a wide variety of other iterable objects.

Example:

original_list = [1, 2, 3]

copy_of_list = list(original_list)

or equivalently

copy_of_list = original_list.copy()

You can use the list() constructor to iterate over the elements of an iterable and create a new list based on a specific condition:

Example:

numbers = list(x for x in range(10) if x % 2 == 0) # Output: [0, 2, 4, 6, 8]

This example creates a list of even numbers from 0 to 9 using a generator expression inside the list() constructor.

When dealing with nested iterables, the list() constructor can be used to flatten the structure:

Example

nested_list = [[1, 2, 3], [4, 5, 6], [7, 8, 9]]

flattened_list = list(item for sublist in nested_list for item in sublist)

Output: [1, 2, 3, 4, 5, 6, 7, 8, 9]

(iii) Building Lists with List Comprehensions

List comprehensions are a concise and powerful feature in Python that allows you to create lists using a compact syntax. They provide a way to build lists by specifying the elements you want to include and the conditions they must meet. Let's explore how to use list comprehensions to construct lists efficiently.

Syntax:

The basic structure of a list comprehension consists of an expression followed by a for clause and, optionally, one or more if clauses. The general syntax is as follows:

[expr(item) for item in iterable]

It needs at least three components:

- **expr()** is a Python expression that returns a concrete value. it should not have to be a function.
- **item** is the current object from iterable.
- **iterable** can be a list, tuple, set, string, or generator.
- **condition (optional):** A condition that filters elements based on a specified criterion.

While expression(item) returns the matching list item that comes from executing the comprehension, the for construct iterates across the items in iterable.

Example:

print([no* 2 for no in range(1, 11)])

[2, 4, 6, 8, 10, 12, 14, 16, 18, 20]

In this example, we use range () to get integer numbers. The comprehension iterates over them while computing the product and building the new list. List comprehensions provide a concise and readable way to build lists in Python. They are a powerful tool for expressing complex transformations and filtering operations in a single line of code. By mastering list comprehensions, you can write more efficient and expressive Python code.

3.1.2 Finding the size of List

In Python, you can find the size of a list using the len() function. The len() function returns the number of elements in an object, and when applied to a list, it provides the size or length of that list. Here's an example:

```
my_list = [1, 2, 3, 4, 5]
# Find the size of the list
list_size = len(my_list)
print("Size of the list:", list_size)
```

In this example, len(my_list) returns the number of elements in the list my_list, and the result is printed. This is a simple and straightforward way to determine the size of a list.

It's important to note that the size of the list corresponds to the number of elements it contains, not the memory size it occupies. If you need information about the memory usage of a list, you might want to consider using the sys.getsizeof() function from the sys module. Keep in mind that getsizeof() returns the size in bytes, and it includes the overhead of the list object itself, not just the elements.

Example:

```
import sys
my_list = [1, 2, 3, 4, 5]
# Find the memory size of the list in bytes
list_memory_size = sys.getsizeof(my_list)
print("Memory size of the list:", list_memory_size, "bytes")
```

This will give you an idea of the memory consumption of the list. Remember that the memory size reported by getsizeof() includes not only the elements of the list but also the memory used by the list object.

3.1.3 Using type()

The type() function in Python is used to get the type of an object. When applied to a list, it returns the type of the list. Here's an example of how you can use type() with a list:

Example:

```
my_list = [1, 2, 3, 4, 5]
# Using type() to get the type of the list
list_type = type(my_list)
print("Type of the list:", list_type)
```

In this example, type(my_list) returns the type of the my_list object, which is <class 'list'>. The result is then printed. The type() function can be useful when you want to check the type of an object dynamically in your code. It's commonly used in scenarios where you need to perform different actions based on the type of an object.

3.1.4 Accessing Items in a List: Indexing

In Python, you can access individual items in a list using indexing. Indexing allows you to retrieve a specific element from a list based on its position. The index is a numeric value representing the position of the element in the list. Python uses zero-based indexing, meaning the first element has an index of 0, the second has an index of 1, and so on.

Example:

Basic List Indexing:

```
my_list = [10, 20, 30, 40, 50]
    # Accessing the first element
first_element = my_list[0]
print("First element:", first_element) # Output: 10
    # Accessing the third element
third_element = my_list[2]
print("Third element:", third_element) # Output: 30
    Negative Indexing:
```

Python also supports negative indexing, where -1 represents the last element, -2 the second-to-last, and so forth:

```
    # Accessing the last element
last_element = my_list[-1]
print("Last element:", last_element) # Output: 50
    # Accessing the second-to-last element
second_to_last = my_list[-2]
print("Second-to-last element:", second_to_last) # Output: 40
    Handling Index Errors
```

Be cautious to avoid index errors by ensuring the index is within the valid range:

```
    # Incorrect: IndexError - list index out of range
# invalid_index = my_list[10]
    # Correct: Check the length of the list before accessing
if len(my_list) > 10:
valid_index = my_list[10]
else:
print("Index out of range")
```

Understanding list indexing is essential for working with lists in Python, as it enables you to access and manipulate individual elements efficiently.

3.1.5 Slicing of List

With the start and end points of the range specified, we can define a range of indexes. A new list containing the provided items will be the return value when a range is specified. A colon(:) can be used to execute a slice operation on lists.

Syntax:

list_object[start:stop:step]

• start indicates the index at which slicing is done. The item at this index is included in the resulting slice.

• stop indicates the index at which the item extraction process ends. The item at this index is not included in the resulting slice.

• step gives an integer value that indicates how many items each step of the slicing will skip. The omitted components won't be included in the final slice.

Example

Return the third, fourth, and fifth item:

L1 = ["a", "b", "c", "d", "e", "f", "g"]

print(L1[2:5])

['c', 'd', 'e']

To print items up until the point of use from a particular index

[index:]

To print the entire list backwards, do

[::-1]

To print items starting at index-1, do:

[: index]

3.1.6 Changing Item Value

To modify an individual item's value, usethe index number

Example:

Change the third item:

L1 = ["a", "b", "c", "d", "e", "f", "g"]

L1[3] = "dd"

print(L1)

['a', 'b', 'c', 'dd', 'e', 'f', 'g']

3.1.7 Changing a Range of Item Values

In order to modify a certain range of items, we must first build a list with the new values and indicate the range of index numbers in the original list where the new values should be inserted.

Example 1
L1 = [10,20,30,40,50,60,70]
L1[1:3] = [25,35]
print(L1)
[10, 25, 35, 40, 50, 60, 70]
Example 2
The example below will change the value in the second index with *two* new values
L1 = [10,20,30,40,50,60,70]
L1[1:2] = [25,35]
print(L1)
[10, 25, 35, 30, 40, 50, 60, 70]
Note: The new things will be placed where you indicated and the remaining items will shift correspondingly if we attempt to introduce fewer items than you replace.

Example3
Replace the values for the second and third with the same value:
L1 = [10,20,30,40,50,60,70]
L1[1:3] = [25]
print(L1)
[10, 25, 40, 50, 60, 70]

3.1.8 Concatenating Lists

In Python, you can concatenate (combine) two or more lists using the + operator or the extend() method. Both methods result in a new list without modifying the original lists. Let's explore both approaches:

Using the + Operator:
list1 = [1, 2, 3]
list2 = [4, 5, 6]
# Concatenate lists using the + operator
concatenated_list = list1 + list2
print("List 1:", list1)
print("List 2:", list2)
print("Concatenated List:", concatenated_list)

Output:
List 1: [1, 2, 3]
List 2: [4, 5, 6]
Concatenated List: [1, 2, 3, 4, 5, 6]

Using the extend() Method:
list1 = [1, 2, 3]
list2 = [4, 5, 6]
# Concatenate lists using the extend() method
list1.extend(list2)
print("List 1:", list1)
print("List 2:", list2)

Output:
List 1: [1, 2, 3, 4, 5, 6]
List 2: [4, 5, 6]

3.1.9 Repetitions on List

Repetition is the process of replicating a list's contents a certain number of times. The repetition operator (*) with two operands allows us to accomplish this. The list whose content needs to be repeated is the first operand. The second operand is used to specify the number of times we need repetitions.
Example
print(["E", "A", "G"] * 4)
['E', 'A', 'G', 'E', 'A', 'G', 'E', 'A', 'G', 'E', 'A', 'G']

3.1.10 Finding Items in a List

Python's membership operators of in and not in let us search for values within an existing list.
Example
l=[10,20,30,40,50]
print(10 in l)
print(60 not in l)
True
True

Note. Membership operators will return Boolean values True and False. The element's presence in the list can be determined using the in operator, and its absence can be determined using the not in operator. These are just a few examples, and the method you choose depends on your specific use case. The in operator is simple and effective for basic checks, while the index() method provides the index of the first occurrence. Looping through the list allows for more complex conditions and actions.

3.1.11 Finding Maximum, and Minimum of a List

The sum of the elements in a list, minimum element and maximum element can be found using sum().max() and min() function respectively. The argument of these functions are the list for which we want to perform the operation

Example:

```
li1=[11,22,33,44,55]
print(min(li1))
print(max(li1))
print(sum(li1))
11
55
165
```

3.1.12 Comparison among Lists

In general, we might have to compare the lists. List objects are compatible with the common comparison operators.

Example

```
list1=[1,2]
list2=[1,2]
list3=[3,4]
print(list1==list2)
print(list1!=list3)
print(list1<list2)
print(list1<list3)
True
True
False
```

True
Element-wise Comparison:
When using equality (==), the order and values of elements must be the same for both lists.
Lexicographical Comparison:
The lexicographical comparison (<, <=, >, >=) compares lists element-wise until a difference is found.
Membership Check:
The membership check (in and not in) can be used for both checking if a list is a subset and if an element is present in another list.
Choose the comparison method that best suits your specific use case, considering the requirements for equality and the desired comparison logic

3.1.13 Loop with list

Looping through a list is a common operation in Python and can be done using various constructs such as for loops. Here are a few examples:
Examples
Using a for Loop:
Products = ["Paper", "Pen", "Pencil"]
for x in Products:
print(x)
Paper
Pen
Pencil
Looping with Indices:
Products = ["Paper", "Pen", "Pencil"]
for x in range(len(Products)):
print(Products[x])
Paper
Pen
Pencil
l= [1,2,3,4,5,6]
j= 0
while j< len(l):
print(l[j])
j= j + 1
Output

1
2
3
4
5
6

Enumerating Elements:

The enumerate() function allows you to iterate through both the indices and elements of a list simultaneously:

my_list = [1, 2, 3, 4, 5]

Enumerate over the elements

for index, value in enumerate(my_list):

print(f"Index: {index}, Value: {value}")

3.1.14 List Methods

Lists are versatile data structures, and they come with a variety of built-in methods that facilitate common operations. Here are some commonly used list methods:

append(*elmnt*)

An element can be added using this to the end of the list.

Example

m1 = ["j", "f", "m"]

m2 = ["a", "m", "j"]

m1.append(m2)

print(m1)

['j', 'f', 'm', ['a', 'm', 'j']]

clear()

Using this method, every element in a list is eliminated.

Example

units = [1,2,3]

units.clear()

print(units)

[]

copy ()

This will create a copy of the list

Example

M1 = ["Jan", "Feb", "Mar"]

```
Newlist=M1.copy()
print(Newlist)
```
['Jan', 'Feb', 'Mar']

count(val)

It is employed to provide the quantity of a given value that occurs. The value to be searched can be of any type (string, number, list, tuple, etc.).

Example
```
marks = [90, 91, 93, 90, 93, 93, 94, 96, 97]
print(marks.count(93))
```
3

extend(iterable)

The supplied list elements, or any iterable, will be appended to the end of the existing list.

Example
```
M1 = ["Jan", "Feb", "Mar"]
M2 = ["Apr", "May", "Jun"]
M1.extend(M2)
print(M1)
```
['Jan', 'Feb', 'Mar', 'Apr', 'May', 'Jun']

index(elmnt)

Its purpose is to locate the point at which the given value appears for the first time.
```
Marks = [40, 57, 78, 32, 8, 45]
print( Marks.index(45))
```
5

insert (pos, elmnt)

It inserts the specified value at the specified position. An element needs to be inserted can be of any type.

Example
```
Mon = ['Jan', 'Mar', 'Apr']
Mon.insert(1, "Feb")
print(Mon)
```
['Jan', 'Feb', 'Mar', 'Apr']

pop([pos])

The element at the given position is removed. Position is optional. Default value is -1 which returns the last item

Example
```
Mon = ['Jan', 'Mar', 'Apr']
```

Mon.pop(1)
print(Mon)
['Jan', 'Apr']
<u>remove ()</u>
The element with the supplied value is removed at the first occurrence.
Example
Mon = ['Jan', 'Mar', 'Apr']
Mon.remove('Mar')
print(Mon)
['Jan', 'Apr']
<u>reverse ()</u>
This method reverses the sorting order of the elements.
Example
Mon = ['Jan', 'Mar', 'Apr']
Mon.reverse()
print(Mon)
['Apr', 'Mar', 'Jan']
Example
<u>sort([reverse=True|False[, key=myFunc]])</u>
This is how the list is sorted. The items will be arranged in ascending order by default.
no = [1,20,11,12,90,34]
no.sort()
print(no)
[1, 11, 12, 20, 34, 90]
Example
no.sort(reverse=True)
[90, 34, 20, 12, 11, 1]

3.2 Python Tuple

A tuple is an ordered collection of immutable Python objects that are separated by commas. It allows duplicates. We use parentheses () to represent Tuples.

3.2.1 Creation of Tuples

We can create the tuples using the following ways

3.2.1.1 Using Literals

```
# Creating a tuple with elements
my_tuple = (1, 2, 3, "hello", 3.14)
    # Creating an empty tuple
empty_tuple = ()
    # Creating a tuple with a single element (note the comma)
single_element_tuple = (42,)
    # Accessing elements in a tuple
print(my_tuple[0]) # Output: 1
print(my_tuple[3]) # Output: hello
    3.2.1.2 Using Constructor
    To create a tuple, you can alternatively use the tuple() constructor.
    # Creating a tuple from a list
my_list = [1, 2, 3]
tuple_from_list = tuple(my_list)
    # Creating a tuple from a string
my_string = "hello"
tuple_from_string = tuple(my_string)
    print(tuple_from_list) # Output: (1, 2, 3)
print(tuple_from_string) # Output: ('h', 'e', 'l', 'l', 'o')
    Combining Tuples:
    tuple1 = (1, 2, 3)
tuple2 = ("a", "b", "c")
    combined_tuple = tuple1 + tuple2
print(combined_tuple)
# Output: (1, 2, 3, 'a', 'b', 'c')
    Nested Tuples:
    Tuples can also be nested, meaning a tuple can contain other tuples:
    nested_tuple = ((1, 2), (3, 4), (5, 6))
    print(nested_tuple[0]) # Output: (1, 2)
print(nested_tuple[1][0]) # Output: 3
    Using Tuple comprehension:
    We can also use comprehension for creating tuples.
    T1 = (1, 2, 3, 4, 5)
    # 'Tuple comprehension'
    mul = tuple(x*2 for x in T1)
```

```
    print(mul)
    (2, 4, 6, 8, 10)
    Unpacking Tuples:
    You can unpack elements of a tuple into separate variables:
    coordinates = (3, 4)
x, y = coordinates
    print("x:", x) # Output: x: 3
print("y:", y) # Output: y: 4
```

Tuples are often used when the order of elements matters, and you want to create an immutable collection of items. They are commonly employed in functions to return multiple values. Understanding tuple creation and manipulation is fundamental for effective Python programming.

3.2.2 Accessing elements in Tuple

Like Lists, There are three methods available to us for gaining access to elements within a tuple: (i) indexing, (ii) reverse indexing, and (iii) utilizing the slice operator. As seen in the sample below, we must include that index number in square brackets for indexing the tuple

(i) Indexing

```
t1 = ('Chennai', 'Bangolore', 'Kolkatta')
    print (t1[0])
    Chennai
```

(ii) Reverse indexing

Starting with the final element, the items are indexed in reverse order. Here, the last element is represented by the indexes −1, −2, −3, and so forth. In the above example t1[-1] represents kolkatta

-5	-4	-3	-2	-1
H	E	L	L	0
0	1	2	3	4

(iii) Slicing

Several components of the tuple are extractable. In order to accomplish this, we use a colon (:) between the index up to the desired point of slicing and the index from which we wish to start.

Example
```
T1 = (11,22,33,44,55,66)
print(T1[1:]) # till end
print(T1[2:4]) # index 2 and 3
print(T1[:4]) # from 0 to 3
print(T1[-4:-1])
print(T1[0::2])
```
Output:
```
(22, 33, 44, 55, 66)
(33, 44)
(11, 22,33, 44)
(33, 44, 55)
(11, 33, 55)
```

3.2.3 Tuple Length

The len() function can be used to determine a tuple's length based on how many items it contains.
```
t = (10,20,30,40,50)
print(len(t1))
5
```

3.2.4 Loop using the Index Numbers

Using the index number of each tuple item, we can also loop through them. Utilizing the range() and len() functions, an appropriate iterable is created.

Example
```
T2 = ("Orange", "Apple", "Banana")
n=len(T2)
for j in range(n):
print(T2[j])
Orange
Apple
Banana
```

3.2.5 Update Tuple using List

Once a tuple is generated, it is not able to add or remove elements since tuples are immutable. However, by using the list() function to turn the tuple into a list, altering the list, and then using the tuple() function to convert the modified list back into a tuple, we may accomplish the aforementioned tasks using lists.

Example
```
m = (10, 30, 30)
y = list(m)
y[1] = 20
m = tuple(y)
print(m)
(10, 20, 30)
```

3.2.6 Add Items

```
m = (10, 20, 30)
y = list(m)
y.append(40)
m = tuple(y)
print(m)
(10, 20, 30, 40)
```

3.2.7 Merging two tuples

```
X = ("che", "Hyd", "Ban")
   Y = ("Mum",)
   X= X+Y
   print(X)
```
('che', 'Hyd', 'Ban', 'Mum')
```
Tu1 = ("a", "b" , "c")
Tu2 = (1, 2, 3)
Tu3 = Tu1 + Tu2
print(Tu3)
```
('a', 'b', 'c', 1, 2, 3)
```
N = (10, 20, 30)
M = N * 3
print(M)
```
(10, 20, 30, 10, 20, 30, 10, 20, 30)

3.2.8 Unpacking a Tuple

Tuple allows us to assign the tuple items into variables through unpacking.

Example
```
Capitals = ("Mumbai","Jaipur","Chennai","Lucknow")
(Maharashtra, Rajasthan, TamilNadu, UttarPradesh) =Capitals
print(Maharashtra)
print(TamilNadu)
print(Rajasthan)
Mumbai
Chennai
Jaipur
```
If the variable name contains a *, then the values will be assigned to it as a list in the event that the number of variables is less than the number of values.

Example
```
No = (1, 20, 21, 22, 345)
(singledigit, *Twodigit, Threedigit) = No
print(singledigit)
print(Twodigit)
print(Threedigit)
```

1
[20, 21, 22]
345
Example
No = (1, 20, 212, 224, 345)
(singledigit, Twodigit, *Threedigit) = No
print(singledigit)
print(Twodigit)
print(Threedigit)
1
20
[212, 224, 345]

3.2.9 Nesting of Tuples

In Python, a tuple within another tuple is referred to as a nested tuple.

Example
t1 = (12,"Kumar","II CSE")
t2 = (90,89,99,98,97,96)
t3 = (t1, t2)
print(t3)
((12, 'Kumar', 'II CSE'), (90, 89, 99, 98, 97, 96))

3.2.10 Deleting Python Tuple Elements

t1 = (10,20,30)
print (t1)
del t1
print (t1)
Error will be the output.

3.2.11 Determine Length of a Tuple

We may use Python's len() method and supply the tuple as the input to determine the length of a tuple.

Example
t= ('A', 'B)
l=len(t)

print(l)

2

3.2.12 Tuple Methods

The set of built-in functions that Tuple offers is as follows.

Method Name	Description	Example
count (value)	It is used return the number of times a specified value appears in the tuple.	t = (10, 20, 70, 10, 70, 50, 40) n = t.count(10) print(n) **output** **2**
index(value)	The index () method finds the first occurrence of the given value. The index () method raises an exception if the value is not found.	t = (10, 20, 70, 10, 70, 50, 40) n = t.index(20) print(n) **output** **1**

Sample Programs on Tuples

1.To convert a list to a tuple.

```
l= [5, 10, 15, 20, 25, 30]
print(l)
t = tuple(l)
print(t)
```
Output
```
[5, 10, 15, 20, 25, 30]
(5, 10, 15, 20, 25, 30)
```
2. Write a Python program to reverse a tuple.
```
T1 = ("Python123")
y = reversed(T1)
print(tuple(y))
T2 = (1, 2, 3, 4)
y = reversed(T2)
```

print(tuple(y))

Output

('3','2','1','n', 'o', 'h', 't', 'y', 'P')

(4, 3, 2, 1)

3. Write a Python program to count the elements in a list until an element is a tuple.

l = [10,20,30,40,(10,20),40]

count = 0

for i in l:

if isinstance(i, tuple):

break

count+= 1

print(count)

Output

4

3.3 DICTIONARY IN PYTHON

An effective data structure called a dictionary in Python is comparable to the hash table data structure seen in other languages. A dictionary in Python is a set of key-value pairs. Here the values are mapped to keys. Items in a dictionary are arranged, modifiable, and do not permit duplication.

3.3.1 Creating Dictionary

We can use two main methods to define a dictionary viz., (i) curly braces {}, (ii) using the dict() method. For example we will create two empty dictionaries.

Creating dictionary

D1= {}

D2 = dict()

The above dictionaries are equivalent.

Example

Student = {

"Name": "Rohith",

"Year": "II" ,

"Dept": "CSE",

"Marks": [90, 98, 100,97,96,95]

```
}
print(Student)
```
{'Name': 'Rohith', 'Year': 'II', 'Dept': 'CSE', 'Marks': [90, 98, 100, 97, 96, 95]}

3.3.2 Length of the Dictionary

The size of the dictionary can be found using len() function. For the above example ,

```
n=len(Student)
print(n)
```
4

3.3.3 Using type() method

The type () method would return a dictionary type if the parameter is dictionary.

```
print(type(Student))
```
<class 'dict'>

3.3.4 Accessing the dictionary values

The well-known square brackets and the key can be used to access the dictionary items and get their values.

```
Example
Emp = {"Name": "Siva", "Age": 25, "salary":85000,"Company":"IBM"}
Name=Emp["Name"]
print(Name)
```
Siva

3.3..5 Adding Dictionary Values

There exist several methods for adding dictionary components. One value at a time, the value and the key can be provided. Need to use an index to add dictionary entries one at a time.

```
Example
Dic={}
Dic[0] = 'Python'
```

```
Dic[1] = 'Java'
Dic[2] = 'C++'
print("\nDictionary after adding 3 elements: ")
print(Dic)
```

Dictionary after adding 3 elements:
{0: 'Python', 1: 'Java', 2: 'C++'}

3.3.6 Adding set of values

We can also add a set of values in dictionary.

```
Dict["Cost"] = 250.00, 300.00, 240.00
print("\nDictionary after adding 3 elements: ")
print(Dict)
```

{0: 'Python', 1: 'Java', 2: 'C++', 'Cost': (250.0, 300.0, 240.0)}

3.3.7 Updating existing Key's Value

The existing element in the dictionary can also be updated by specifying the index or key.

```
Dict[2] = 'Javascript'
print(Dict)
```

{0: 'Python', 1: 'Java', 2: 'Javascript', 'Cost': (250.0, 300.0, 240.0)}

3.3.8 Delete an element

The following instruction explains how to use the del keyword to remove vocabulary elements.

```
del Dictionary_name
```

3.3.9 Iterating through the Dictionary

As seen below, a for loop may be used to run through a dictionary.

Example

```
#To get the keys
Student = {
"Name": "Rohith",
"Year": "II" ,
"Dept": "CSE",
```

```
"Marks": [90, 98, 100,97,96,95]
}
for p in Student:
print(p)
```

Name

Year

Dept

Marks

Example2

```
#Getting the values of keys
Student = {
"Name": "Rohith",
"Year": "II" ,
"Dept": "CSE",
"Marks": [90, 98, 100,97,96,95]
}
for x in Student:
print(Student[x])
```

Rohith

II

CSE

[90, 98, 100, 97, 96, 95]

Example 3

```
#To get both keys and values
Student = {
"Name": "Rohith",
"Year": "II" ,
"Dept": "CSE",
"Marks": [90, 98, 100,97,96,95]
}
for x in Student.items():
print(x)
```

('Name', 'Rohith')

('Year', 'II')

('Dept', 'CSE')

('Marks', [90, 98, 100, 97, 96, 95])

Example 4

```
#Getting keys and values
```

for x,y in Student.items():
print(x,y)
Name Rohith
Year II
Dept CSE
Marks [90, 98, 100, 97, 96, 95]

3.3.10 Nested Dictionaries

Nested dictionaries are dictionaries that are included within other dictionaries.

Method1 : Make a dictionary with the following two dictionaries

Toppers = {
"stud1" : {
"name" : "John",
"mark" : 100
},
"stud2" : {
"name" : "Krishna",
"mark" : 99
}
}

Method 2 : Make one dictionary that will include the other three dictionaries after creating the following three:

stud1= {
"name" : "John",
"mark" : 100
}
stud2= {
"name" : "Krishna",
"mark" : 99
}
stud3 = {
"name" : "Reena",
"mark" : 98
}
Toppers= {
"Stud1" : stud1,

```
"Stud2" : stud2,
"Stud3" : stud3
}
print(Toppers)
```

{'Stud1': {'name': 'John', 'mark': 95}, 'Stud2': {'name': 'Krishna', 'mark': 99}, 'Stud3': {'name': 'Reena', 'mark': 100}}

3.3.11 Dictionary Comprehension

Python makes dictionary comprehensions feasible by enabling us to create dictionaries using simple expressions.

Syntax:

{k: value for (k, val) in iterable}

Where k and val are key and value respectively.

Example

Dict1 = {y: y*2 for y in [10,20,30,40,50]}

print (Dict1)

{10: 20, 20: 40, 30: 60, 40: 80, 50: 100}

3.3.12 Dictionary Membership Test

We may test if the key is in the dictionary or not by using the membership operators in and not in, respectively.

Example

Dict1={1: 2, 2: 4, 3: 6, 4: 8, 5: 10, 6: 12, 7: 14, 8: 16, 9: 18, 10: 20}

print(2 in Dict1)

print(11 not on Dict1)

True

True

3.3.13 Built-in methods

The following built-in Dictionary features are available for use.

Method Name	Description	Example with output
clear()	This will remove all the elements from a dictionary.	Dict1.clear()

copy()	It is used to return a copy of the specified dictionary.	Book = {
		　"Name": "Python",
		　"Price": 400.00,
		　"Quantity": 50
		}
		B1 = Book.copy()
		print(B1)
		>>>> {'Name': 'Python', 'Price': 400.0, 'Quantity': 50}

dict.fromkeys (keys, value)	It can return a dictionary with the specified keys and the specified value. Keys: An iterable specifying the keys of the new dictionary Value: The value for all keys. Default value is None	b=("C","Python") c=100 B2=dict.fromkeys(b,c) print(B2) >>>>{'C': 100, 'Python': 100} b=("C","Python") B2=dict.fromkeys(b) print(B2) >>>> {'C': None, 'Python': None}

get(keyname[, value])	This will return the value of the item with the specified key.
	
	The key name of the item you want to return the value from
	A value to return if the specified key does not exist. Default value None
		Book = {
		　"Name": "Python",
		　"Price": 400.00,
		　"Quantity": 50
		}
		
		print(Book.get("Name"))
		>>>Pyhton

items()	It is used to create a view object. The view object contains the key-value pairs of the dictionary, as tuples in a list.
	
	Remember: When an item in the dictionary changes value, the view object also gets updated:
		Book = {
		　"Name": "Python",
		　"Price": 400.00,
		　"Quantity": 50
		}
		B=Book.items()
		print("Before updation of Quantity")
		print(B)
		Book["Quantity"]=100
		print("After Updation of Quantity")
		print(B)
		>>Before updation of Quantity
		dict_items([('Name', 'Python'), ('Price', 400.0), ('Quantity', 50)])
		After Updation of Quantity

3.3.14 Choosing right data structure

The rules to choose one of these data structures are simple:

1. When we need a sequence of elements that you can access with indexing, we can choose a list.
2. If we need to quickly access an element mapped to a specific unique key, then we can choose a dictionary.

Summary

- List is used to store the list of elements of any data type. It has slicing and various methods to manipulate the elements.
- Tuple is used to store the list of elements of any data type. But it won't allow duplicate values.
- Dictionary is used to store key and value pair to avoid the direct access of values.

## CHAPTER FOUR

Strings and Functions

A String is an immutable sequence data type in python, composed of a collection of characters. It can include alphabets, numbers, and even special characters. Since the string is immutable , it can't be changed.

4.1 String Creation

To express a string literal, enclose a string of characters in a single quotation ('Welcome'), double quotes ("Welcome"), or triple quotes ('''Welcome''').

4.2 Assigning string literal to the variable

A variable can be assigned with string literal using an equal sign.
Example
Program
fruit = "Apple"
print(fruit)
Output
Apple
To check the type of variable fruit, type function with string variable as argument
Program
fruit = "Apple"
print(type(Fruit))
Output
<class 'str'>
Program
str='''A multiline strings are assigned to the
Variable using a pair of

triple quotes"'
print(str)
Output
A multiline strings are assigned to the
Variable using a pair of
triple quotes

4.3 Accessing values in string

An organized group of things is referred by the term "sequence".Thus, a string is just a collection of characters. The sequence uses an index that starts at zero to obtain a specific item.

The final character is located at len (String)-1's index.Strings in Python are collection of bytes that correspond to Unicode characters.. Applications are free to utilize any of these countless character combinations since Python's string type uses the Unicode Standard to represent characters. A single character is represented as a string of length 1 in Python as the language does not provide character data types.

String elements can be accessed using square brackets [].
Program
str1="Hello World"
print(str1[0])
print(str1[6])
Output
H
W

4.3.1 String Slicing

String slicing is the process by which a user extracts substrings from a string.. String indexing and slicing in Python are performed by specifying the start and stop indices within square brackets ([ ]).

Syntax

string[start:stop:stride]

- string: The variable or string literal that you want to slice.

- start: The index at which the slicing should begin. This position is inclusive in the slice.
- stop: The index at which the slicing should end. This position is exclusive in the slice.
- stride (optional): The step size or the number of characters to skip between each character in the resulting substring.
- The part of Str1 that starts at position p and goes up to but does not include location q is returned by an expression of the type str1[p:q].

Example
Program
str1="Hello World"
print(str1[3:5])
Output
lo

The first character in the string in the example above has index 0. The length of the substring is q-p. The slice begins at the beginning of the string if the user omits p. Str1[:q] and Str1[0:q] are hence equal. Similarly, if user omit q Str1[p:], the slice starts from p index of Str1 to the end of the string.

Example
Program
s1="Hello World"
print(s1[3])
Output
lo World

Now, omitting both p and q returns the original string , will get the entire string.

Program
s1="Python"
print(s1[:])
Output
Python

Remember that if p in a slice is more than or equal to q, Python outputs an empty string.

4.3.2 Negative Index

Slicing can also be done with negative indices. As with basic indexing, -1 denotes the last character, -2 the next-to-last, and so on. The Figure 4.1 shows the negative indexing for the string "welcome".

-7	-6	-5	-4	-3	-2	-1
W	e	l	c	o	m	e
0	1	2	3	4	5	6

Figure 4.1 Negative Indexing

Program
```
str1="welcome"
print(str1[-7:-2])
```
Output
```
welco
```

4.3.2 Specifying a Stride in a String Slice

"Stride" here refers to the step size or the number of characters to skip between each character in the resulting substring. By specifying the stride value in string slicing, you can extract substrings with specific character intervals.

Example
Program
```
st = 'Welcome'
print( st[0:7:2])
print(st[::5])
print(st[4::5])
```
Output
```
Wloe
Wm
o
```

Python can also be used to define a negative stride value, in which case the text is traversed backward. Then, the beginning index (first index) should be higher than the ending index (second index).

Example
Program
s = 'Welcome'
print(s[7:0:-2])
Output
eol

4.4 Modifying Strings

String is immutable datatype in Python. That is, it is impossible to modify the string.

Example
Program
str = "Welcome"
str[0] = "W"
print(str)
Output
Error

However, users can typically achieve what they want with ease by creating a duplicate of the original string with the appropriate modification made.

Example
Program
s = "WELCOME"
print(s)
s = "Welcome to India"
print(s)
Output
WELCOME
Welcome to India

The string "s" in the example above has been completely assigned to a new piece of information as stated. Users can also change the character in a particular index.

Example
Program
s='Toolbar'
s = s[:4] + 'c' + s[5:]

    print(s)
Output
    Toolcar
    To do this, there's also built in string method available:
    Program
    s = 'Toolbar'
    s = s.replace('b', 'c')
    print(s)
Output
    Toolcar

4.4.1 Deleting the String

Users are unable to add or remove characters from strings since they are immutable objects. However, they may use the del keyword to remove the entire string.
    s = 'tool bar'
    del s

4.4.2 Length of the string

The built-in len() method may be used by users to determine the length of a string.
    Program
    str="welcome!"
    print(len(str))
Output
    8

4.4.3 Concatenation of Strings

Python allows us to combine more than one string using + operator.
    Example
    Program
    s1="Hello"
    s2="Welcome"
    s3=s1+" " +s2+"!"

    print(s3)
Output
    Hello Welcome!

4.4.4 Formatting String

Python does not allow to combine strings with other data types. The following code trying to combine string and integer and shows the error.

Example

Program

```
s1="My Registration number is"
s2=1001
s3=s1+" " +s2
print(s3)
```

Output

    Error
    But user can use format method as follows.

Example

Program

```
RegisterNo=1001
s1="My Register No is {}"
print(s1.format(RegisterNo))
```

Output

    My Register No is 1001

4.5 Built in String Methods

Here are some of the more often used built-in operations on string objects that Python offers.

Method name	Description	Example Program with output
capitalize()	It creates a copy of string with the first character in uppercase and every other character in lowercase.	s1 = "python" s2 = s1.capitalize() print (s2) **output** Python
casefold()	It converts string into lower case	s1 = "HELLO" s2 = s1.casefold() print(s2) **output** hello
center(len[, char])	It will return a centered string len specifies length of returned string.	txt1 = "Python" p = txt1.center(30,'x') print(p) **output** xxxxxxxPythonxxxxxxx
count(val[, start[, end]])	This method will return the number of times a specified value occurs in a string.	s1= "Python is a Programming language print(s1.count("Program") **output** 1
endswith(val[, start[, end]])	It returns true if the string ends with the specified value	s1= "Actions speak louder than words." print(s1.endswith("words") **output** True
find(value[, start[, end]])	It will return the index of first occurrence of the specified value.	s1 = "Welcome to Python" s2 = S1.find("P") print(s2) **output** 11
format(val1, val2...)	This is used to format specified values in a string.	s1 = "His name is {name}.He is {age}".f "Raj", age = 21) print(s1) **output** His name is Raj.He is 21
index(value[, start[, end]])	This method is used to searches the string for a specified value and returns the position of where it was found.	str1= "Python" pos= str1.index("t") print(pos) **output** 2
isalnum()	This is used to check all the characters are alphanumeric, meaning alphabet letter (a-z) and numbers (0-9). It will return TRUE if all are alphanumeric otherwise it returns FALSE	s1 = "!w1Apple" s = s1.isalnum() print(s) **output** False
isalpha()	It will return True if all the characters are alphabet letters (a-z). Otherwise, it returns False	s1 = "Banana" print(s1.isalpha()) **output** True
isascii()	It will return true if all characters in the string are ascii characters	s1 = "Welcome to python12" print(s1. isascii()) **output** True
isdecimal()	It returns true if all the characters in the string are decimal digits (0-9)	x= "456" print(x.isdecimal()) **output** True
isdigit()	It returns true if all the characters are digits.	x= "A456" print(x.isdigit()) **output** False
isidentifier()	It returns True if the string is a valid identifier, otherwise False.	w = "Mark" x= "File1" y = "2Name" z = " File Name" print(w.isidentifier()) print(x.isidentifier()) print(y.isidentifier())

4.6 String operators

List of operators used in strings are available in the below table.

Operator	Description
+	It joins the strings given either side of the operator.
*	This repetition operator concatenates the multiple copies of the same string. s='Hello' print(s*3) **output** HelloHelloHello
[]	This will access the sub-strings of a particular string.
[:]	The range slice operator accesses the characters from the specified range.
in	This membership operator is to find sub-string is present in the specified string or not. This will return True if is present. Otherwise, False will be returned. s='Welcome' print('come' in s) **output** True
not in	It does the exact reverse of in. It returns true if a particular substring is not present in the specified string. S='Welcome' print('raj' not in S) **output** True
r/R	It is used to specify the raw string. In Python, a raw string is a special type of string that allows you to include backslashes (\) without interpreting them as escape sequences such as "C://myfolder ". To define any string as a raw string, the character r or R is followed by the string. print(r'C://myfolder') **output** >C://myfolder
%	It is used to perform string formatting. This is similar to the format specifiers used in C programming like %d or %f to map their values in python. s = "Python" print("The string is : %s"%(s)) **output** The string is : Python

4.7 Escape Character

The characters that can't insert into a string are called Illegal characters, and these characters modify the string.

Example

You will get an error if you use double quotes inside a string that is surrounded by double quotes:

txt = "Students need to "create" own study environment"

output

Error

In Python programming, the backslash character enables the program to escape the following characters. Escape sequences allow you to include special characters in strings. To do this, simply add a backslash (\) before the character you want to escape.

Following would be the syntax for an escape sequence

Syntax:

\Escape character

To print " in output ,

txt = "Students need to \"study\" on their own"

The list of escape characters used in Python is given below

Escape Sequence	Meaning
\'	Single Quote
\\	Backslash
\n	New Line
\r	Carriage Return
\t	Tab
\b	Backspace
\f	Form Feed
\ooo	Octal value
\xhh	Hex value

4.8 Functions

A function is a group of computer statements that can be used repeatedly in a program in any programming or scripting language. It helps developers save time. The idea of a function is the same in Python as it is in other languages. Some built-in functions are included with Python. In addition, users can define functions based on our needs.

4.8.1 Function Definition and Call

The term def and the function name come first in the declaration of a user-defined function in Python. Within the opening and closing parentheses, immediately following the function name followed by a colon, the function may accept one or more arguments as input. The next line should begin with a block of program statements that are indented after defining the function name and argument(s). The syntax of a user-defined function is seen below.

def function_name(argument1, argument2, ...) :
statement_1
statement_2
....
function_name(arg1, arg2)
Example
Program
def my_function():
print("Hello from a function")
my_function()
output
Hello from a function

4.8.2 Function with Arguments

An argument in computer programming is a value that a function will accept.

Program
def addition(a, b):
sum = a + b
print('Sum is', sum)
addition(7, 3)
output
Sum is 10

4.8.3 Lambda Functions

In Python, a lambda function is a special type of function without the function name. Use the lambda keyword instead of def to create a lambda function. Here's the syntax to declare the lambda function:

Syntax

lambda argument(s) : expression

Here,

argument(s) - any value passed to the lambda function

expression - expression is executed and returned

Example

Program

```
double = lambda x: x * 3
print(double(2))
```

output

```
6
```

The following user defined functions is similar to the above lambda function.

Program

```
def double(x):
return x * 3
x=double(2)
print(x)
```

output

```
6
```

4.8.4 Function Default Arguments

In the user defined function, users can set the default value for the arguments.

Program

```
def message(name, msg="Good morning!"):
print("Hello", name + ', ' + msg)
message("raj")
message("raj", "How do you do?")
```

output

```
Hello raj, Good morning!
Hello raj, How do you do?
```

Example

Users can use tuple data type with the user defined function. The demonstration of printing the list of names using tuple is given below.

Program

*def message(*names):*

for x in names:

print("Hello", x)

mesage("raj", "tabjulu", "ragu", "amit")

output

Hello raj

Hello tabjulu

Hello ragu

Hello amit

4.8.5 Recursive Functions

Recursion is the process of defining something in terms of itself. Recursion is a method for solving computer problems that involves writing a function that calls itself again until the program yields the desired outcome.

Program

def factorial(x):

if x == 1:

return 1

else:

*return (x * factorial(x-1))*

num = 5

print("The factorial of", num, "is", factorial(num))

output

The factorial of 5 is 120

output

Hello raj

Hello tabjulu

Hello ragu

Hello amit

Summary

- String is a sequence of characters, which has many built in methods to manipulate
- Funtion is used to execute the taks repeatedly. It has many forms includes lamda functions and recursive functions.

• 75 •

## CHAPTER FIVE

File Handling

File handling is an integral part of programming. File handling in Python is simplified with built-in methods, which include creating, opening, and closing files. While files are open, Python additionally allows performing various file operations, such as reading, writing, and appending information.

5.1 Opening Files in Python

The open() Python method is the primary file handling function. The basic syntax is:

file_object = open('file_name', 'mode')

The open() function takes two elementary parameters for file handling:

1. The file_name includes the file extension and assumes the file is in the current working directory. If the file location is elsewhere, provide the absolute or relative path.

2. The mode is an optional parameter that defines the file opening method. The table below outlines the different possible options.

Mode	Description
'r'	Reads from a file and returns an error if the file does not exist (**default**).
'w'	Writes to a file and creates the file if it does not exist or overwrites an existing file.
'x'	Exclusive creation that fails if the file already exists.
'a'	Appends to a file and creates the file if it does not exist or overwrites an existing file.
'b'	Binary mode. Use this mode for non-textual files, such as images.
't'	Text mode. Use only for textual files (**default**).
'+'	Activates read and write methods.

The mode must have exactly one create(x)/read(r)/write(w)/append(a) method, at most one +. Omitting the mode defaults to 'rt' for reading text files.

5.1.1 Read Mode

The read mode in Python opens an existing file for reading, positioning the pointer at the file's start. To read a text file in Python, load the file by using the open() function:

f = open("<file name>")

The mode defaults to read text ('rt'). Therefore, the following method is equivalent to the default:

f = open("<file name>", "rt")

To read files in binary mode, use:

f = open("<file name>", "rb")

Add + to open a file in read and write mode:

f = open("<file name>", "r+") # Textual read and write

f = open("<file name>", "rt+") # Same as above

f = open("<file name>", "rb+") # Binary read and write

In all cases, the function returns a file object and the characteristics depend on the chosen mode.

5.1.2 Write Mode

Write mode creates a file for writing content and places the pointer at the start. If the file exists, write truncates (clears) any existing information.

To open a file for writing information, use:

f = open("<file name>", "w")

f = open("<file name>", "wt")

f = open("<file name>", "wb")

Add + to allow reading the file:

f = open("<file name>", "w+") # Textual write and read

f = open("<file name>", "wt+") # Same as above

f = open("<file name>", "wb+") # Binary write and read

The **open()** function returns a file object whose details depend on the chosen modes.

5.1.3 Append Mode

Append mode adds information to an existing file, placing the pointer at the end. If a file does not exist, append mode creates the file.

The key difference between write and append modes is that append does not clear a file's contents.

f = open("<file name>", "a") # Text append

f = open("<file name>", "at") # Same as above

f = open("<file name>", "ab") # Binary append

Add the + sign to include the read functionality.

5.1.4 Create Mode

Create mode (also known as exclusive create) creates a file only if it doesn't exist, positioning the pointer at the start of the file.

If the file exists, Python throws an error. Use this mode to avoid overwriting existing files.

f = open("<file name>", "x") # Text create

f = open("<file name>", "xt") # Same as above

f = open("<file name>", "xb") # Binary create

Add the + sign to the mode include reading functionality to any of the above lines.

5.2 Reading Files in Python

After importing a file into an object, Python offers numerous methods to read the contents. Use the read() method on the file object and print the result. For example:

f = open("file.txt")

print(f.read(),end="")

The print() function automatically adds a new empty line. To change this behavior, add the end="" parameter to print() to remove the empty line.

f=open("file.txt")

print(f.read(),end="")

5.2.1 Read Parts of the File

Provide a number to the read() function to read only the specified number of characters:

```
f = open("file.txt")
print(f.read(5))
```

The output prints the first five characters in the file. Alternatively, use the readline() method to print only the first line of the file:

```
f = open("file.txt")
print(f.readline())
```

Add an integer to the readline() function to print the specified number of characters without exceeding the first line.

5.2.2 Read Lines

To read lines and iterate through a file's contents, use a for loop:

```
f = open("file.txt")
for line in f:
print(line, end="")
```

Alternatively, use the readlines() method on the file object:

```
f = open("file.txt")
print(f.readlines())
```

The function returns the list of lines from the file stream.

Add an integer to the readlines() function to control the number of lines. For example:

```
f = open("file.txt")
print(f.readlines(15))
```

The integer represents the character number, and the function returns the line where the character ends along with the previous lines.

5.2.3 Close Files

A file remains open until invoking the close() function. It's good practice to close files no longer in use to avoid unpredictable file behavior and corrupted files. To close a file, run the close() method on the file object:

```
f.close()
```

An alternative way to ensure a file closes is to use the with statement. For example:

```
with open("<file name>"):
file_contents = f.read()
```

Additional code here

The with statement automatically closes the file.

5.2.4 Deleting Files in Python

Removing files in Python requires establishing communication with the operating system. Import the os library and delete a file with the following:

```
import os
os.remove("file.txt")
```

The file is no longer available. If the file does not exist, Python throws an error.

5.3 Python File Methods

Python offers various other functions when working with file objects. Below is a table that outlines all available processes and what they do.

Sl.no	Method	Description
1	close()	Flushes and closes the file object.
2	detach()	Separates buffer from text stream and returns the buffer.
3	fileno()	Returns the file's descriptor if available.
4	flush()	Flushes the write buffer. Not available for read-only objects.
5	isatty()	Checks if a file stream is interactive.
6	read(<int>)	Read <int> number of characters at most.
7	readable()	Checks if an object is readable.
8	readline(<int>)	Reads from the object until a newline or end of the file.
9	readlines(<int>)	Returns a list of lines from the file object, where <int> is the approximate character number.
10	seek(<offset>, <position>)	Changes the pointer position to <offset> relative to the <position>.
11	seekable()	Checks if the file object supports random access.
12	tell()	Prints the current stream position.
13	truncate(<byte>)	Resizes the file stream to <bytes> (or current position if unstated) and returns the size.
14	write(<string>)	Writes <string> to the file object and returns the written number of characters.
15	writable()	Checks whether the file object allows writing.
16	writelines(<list>)	Writes a <list> of lines to the stream without a line separator.

5.4 Seek()

In Python, seek() function is used to change the position of the File Handle to a given specific position. File handle is like a cursor, which defines from where the data has to be read or written in the file.

5.5 Tell()

Tells the current position of the pointer in a file

tell() and seek()

```
f = open("sample.txt", "r")
f.seek(20)
print(f.tell())
print(f.readline())
f.close()
```

Summary

- Python File handling has different modes.
- Basically, it will do three activities viz., read,write and append
- tell and seek are the important methods in file handling to change the position and current position .

## CHAPTER SIX

Practice Programs

#Program 1 Find the area of circle

```
r=float(input("Enter radius of circle:-"))
area=(22/7)*r*r
print("Area is",area,"units")
```

#Program 2 FInd the area of the rectangle

```
l=float(input("Enter length of rectangle:-"))
b=float(input("Enter breadth of rectangle:-"))
area=l*b
print("Area is",area,"units")
```

#Program 3 Find the given number is positive or negative

```
n=float(input("Enter number other than 0 to check positive or negative:-"))
if(n>0):
print(n,"is Positive")
else:
print(n,"is Negative")
```

#Program 4 Find the given number is positive or negative or zero

```
n=float(input("Enter number to check positive, negative, or zero:-"))
if(n>0):
print(n,"is Positive")
elif(n<0):
print(n,"is Negative")
else:
print(int(n),"is Zero")
```

#Program 5 print the numbers from 1 to 100

```
i=1
while(i<=100):
print(i)
```

```python
i=i+1
```

#Program 6 Print the numbers from 100 to 1

```python
i=100
while(i>=1):
print(i)
i=i-1
```

#Program 7 Find the sum of digits of a given number

```python
n=float(input("Enter a number to find sum of digits:-"))
sum=0.0
while(n>=1):
r=n%10
sum=sum+r
n=int(n/10)
print(sum)
```

#Program 8 To reverse a given number

```python
n=int(input("Enter the number to reverse:-"))
rn=0
while(n>0):
r=n%10
rn=rn*10+r
n=int(n/10)
print(rn)
```

#Program 9 to find the given number is palindrome or not

```python
n=int(input("Enter a number to check palindrome:-"))
on=n
rn=0
while(n>0):
r=n%10
rn=rn*10+r
n=int(n/10)
if(rn==on):
print(on,"is a Palindrome")
else:
print(on,"is not a Palindrome")
```

#Program 10 to find the given number is armstrong or not

```python
n=int(input("Enter a number to check if it is Armstrong number:-"))
on=n
soc=0
```

```python
while(n>0):
r=int(n%10)
soc=soc+r*r*r
n=int(n/10)
if(soc==on):
print(on,"is an Armstrong number")
else:
print(on,"is not an Armstrong number")
```

#Program 11 print the numbers from 1 to 100 which are divisble by 6

```python
i=1
while(i<=100):
if((i%6)==0):
print(i)
i=i+1
```

#Program 12 swap two numbers using third variable

```python
a=int(input("Enter the first number:-"))
b=int(input("Enter the second number:-"))
temp=a
a=b
b=temp
print(a,b)
```

#Program 13 swap two numbers without using third variable

```python
a=int(input("Enter the first number:-"))
b=int(input("Enter the second number:-"))
a=a+b
b=a-b
a=a-b
print(a,b)
```

#Program 14 check the biggest among two numbers

```python
a=int(input("Enter the first number:-"))
b=int(input("Enter the second number:-"))
if(a==b):
print(a,"and",b,"are equal")
elif(a>b):
print(a,"is larger than",b)
else:
print(b,"is larger than",a)
```

#Program 15 Biggest among three numbers

```
a=int(input("Enter the first number:-"))
b=int(input("Enter the second number:-"))
c=int(input("Enter the third number:-"))
if((a==b)&(b==c)):
print(a,"and",b,"and",c,"are equal")
elif((a>b)&(a>c)):
print(a,"is the biggest")
elif((b>c)and(b>a)):
print(b,"is the biggest")
else:
print(c,"is the biggest")
```

#Program 16 Biggest among ten numbers

```
a=[]
i=0
while(i<10):
n=int(input("Enter the element"))
a.append(n)
i=i+1
print(a)
big=a[0]
i=1
while(i<10):
if(a[i]>big):
big=a[i]
i=i+1
print("biggest is",big)
```

#Program 17 Biggest among n numbers

```
a=[]
i=0
n=int(input("Enter the n value"))
while(i<n):
nl=int(input("Enter the element"))
a.append(nl)
i=i+1
print(a)
big=a[0]
i=1
while(i<n):
```

```
if(a[i]>big):
big=a[i]
i=i+1
print("biggest is",big)
```

#program 18 Check the number of zeros in a given number

```
n=int(input("Enter the number to check zeroes:"))
c=0
while(n>0):
d=n%10
if(d==0):
c=c+1
n=n//10
print(c,"zeroes are present")
```

#program 19 Print he odd numbers from 1 to 100 using for loop

```
for i in range(1,100,2):
print(i)
```

#program 20

```
a=[]
i=0
n=int(input("Enter the number of elements:"))
while(i<n):
n1=int(input("Enter the number:"))
a.append(n1)
i=i+1
i=0
while(i<n):
j=i+1
while(j<n):
if(a[i]>a[j]):
temp=a[i]
a[i]=a[j]
a[j]=temp
j=j+1
i=i+1
print(a)
```

#Program 21 print the factorial of a given number

```
n=int(input())
fact=1
```

```
i=1
if (n==0)or(n==1):
print(fact)
else:
while(i<=n):
fact=fact*i
i=i+1
print(fact)
```

#Program 22 Print the fibonacci series of a given input

```
n=int(input("Enter the number of terms:"))
n1,n2=0,1
i=1
if(n<=0):
print("No series")
elif(n==1):
print("0")
else:
while(i<=n):
print(n1,end=" ")
n3=n1+n2
n1=n2
n2=n3
i=i+1
```

#Program 23 print the matrix for the given number of rows and columns

```
a=[]
m=int(input("Enter the number of rows:"))
n=int(input("Enter the number of columns:"))
for i in range(0,m):
v1=[]
for j in range(0,n):
no=int(input("Enter element:"))
v1.append(no)
a.append(v1)
print()
for i in range(0,m):
for j in range(0,n):
print(a[i][j],end="\t")
```

```
print()
print()
#Program 24 Peform addition of two 3X3 matrices
a=[]
b=[]
for i in range(0,3):
v1=[]
for j in range(0,3):
no=int(input("Enter element:"))
v1.append(no)
a.append(v1)
for i in range(0,3):
v1=[]
for j in range(0,3):
no=int(input("Enter element:"))
v1.append(no)
b.append(v1)
for i in range(0,3):
for j in range(0,3):
b[i][j]=a[i][j]+b[i][j]
print()
for i in range(0,3):
for j in range(0,3):
print(b[i][j],end="\t")
print()
print()
#Program 25 perform multiplication of two 3X3 matrices
a=[]
b=[]
c=[]
for i in range(0,3):
v1=[]
v2=[]
for j in range(0,3):
no=int(input("Enter element:"))
v1.append(no)
v2.append(0)
a.append(v1)
```

```python
c.append(v2)
print(c,"will store final matrice")
for i in range(0,3):
v1=[]
for j in range(0,3):
no=int(input("Enter element:"))
v1.append(no)
b.append(v1)
for i in range(0,3):
for j in range(0,3):
for k in range(0,3):
c[i][j]=c[i][j]+a[i][k]*b[k][j]
print()
for i in range(0,3):
for j in range(0,3):
print(c[i][j],end="\t")
print()
print()
```

#Program 26 print the number of lower case letters in a given string
```python
s=input()
lower=0
for i in s:
if(i>='a'and i<='z'):
lower=lower+1
print(lower)
```

#Program 27 print the number of uppercase and lowercase letters in a given string
```python
s=input()
lower,upper=0,0
for i in s:
if(i>='a'and i<='z'):
lower=lower+1
elif(i>="A" and i<="Z"):
upper=upper+1
print(lower)
print(upper)
```

#Program 28 print the number of uppercase,lowercase letters and digits in a given string

```
s=input()
lower,upper,dig=0,0,0
for i in s:
if(i>='a'and i<='z'):
lower=lower+1
elif(i>="A" and i<="Z"):
upper=upper+1
elif(i>='0' and i<='9'):
dig=dig+1
print(lower)
print(upper)
print(dig)
```

#Program 29 print the number of upper,lower,special case letters and digits in a given input

```
s=input()
lower,upper,dig,spec=0,0,0,0
for i in s:
if(i>='a'and i<='z'):
lower=lower+1
elif(i>="A" and i<="Z"):
upper=upper+1
elif(i>='0' and i<='9'):
dig=dig+1
elif(i==" "):
continue
else:
spec+=1
print(lower)
print(upper)
print(dig)
print(spec)
```

#Program 30 count the number of characters

```
s=input("Enter the string")
count=0
for i in s:
if i==" ":
continue
count=count+1
```

```
print(count)
#using Inbuilt Function
count1=len(s)
print(count1)
```

#Program 31 convert the string into lower case letters

```
s=input("Enter a string:")
i=0
ch2="
while s[i:]:
"""
: in front of i is for i till end of string
ord function is used for getting ASCII value
"""
ch=ord(s[i])
if ch>64 and ch<91:
ch2+=chr(ch+32)
else:
ch2+=chr(ch)
i+=1
print("Lowercase String is:",ch2)
#using inbuilt function
string='VIT University'
print(string.lower())
```

#Program 32 convert the given string into upper case letters

```
s=input("Enter a string:")
i=0
ch2="
while s[i:]:
ch=ord(s[i])
if ch>96 and ch<123:
ch2+=chr(ch-32)
else:
ch2+=chr(ch)
i+=1
print("Uppercase String is:",ch2)
#uisng inbuilt in function
string='VIT University'
print(string.upper())
```

#Program 33 find the second biggest among n numbers

```
a=[]
i=0
c=0
n=int(input("Enter no of elements:"))
while(i<n):
n1=int(input())
a.append(n1)
i+=1
print(a)
big=a[0]
i=0
while(i<n):
if(a[i]>big):
big=a[i]
i=i+1
print(a)
i=0
if(big==a[0]):
big1=a[1]
else:
big1=a[0]
while(i<n):
if(a[i]>big1 and a[i]!=big):
big1=a[i]
i=i+1
print(big1)
```

#Program 34 demonstration of user defined function

```
def welcome(name):
print("Hello, "+name+". Good Morning!")
welcome("ABC")
```

#Program 35 user defined function

```
def welcome(name, msg="Good morning!"):
print("Hello",name+', '+msg)
welcome("Yadav")
welcome("Gokul", "How do you do?")
```

#Program 36 user defined function

```
t=("partha","sar","welcomes","you")
```

```python
print(t)
def welcome(*names):
for x in names:
print("Hello", x)
welcome("Raj","Tabjulu","Ragu","Amit")
welcome(t)
```

#Program 37-Factorial using user defined function

```python
def factorial(x):
if x==1:
return 1
else:
return(x*factorial(x-1))
n=int(input("Enter a number:"))
z=factorial(n)
print("The factorial of", n, "is", z)
```

#Program 38 Demonstration of lambda function

```python
twice=lambda x:x*2
print(twice(5))
#use filter()
my_list=[1,5,4,6,8,11,3,12]
new_list=list(filter(lambda x: (x%2==0), my_list))
print(new_list)
#use map()
newlist=list(map(lambda x:x*2, my_list))
print(newlist)
```

#Program 39

```python
x="global"
def f():
print("x inside:", x)
f()
print("x outside:", x)
def f1():
y1="local"
print(y1)
f1()
def f2():
x1="local"
print(x1)
```

```python
f2()
```

#Program 40 searching an element in a list

```python
a=[]
i=0
n=int(input("No of elements in list:"))
while(i<n):
ele=int(input("Element of list:"))
a.append(ele)
i=i+1
print(a)
b=int(input("Number to find:"))
i=0
while(i<n):
if(a[i]==b):
print("Found at index", i)
break
i=i+1
```

#Program 44 Demonstration of pattern printing

```python
n=int(input("Enter the number of rows:"))
for i in range(1,n+1):
for j in range(1,n+1):
if j<=i:
print(i,end=" ")
else:
print(j,end=" ")
print()
```

#Program 45 Demonstration of pattern printing

```python
n=int(input("Enter number of rows"))
for i in range(n):
for j in range(i+1):
print("*",end=" ")
print()
```

www.ingramcontent.com/pod-product-compliance
Lightning Source LLC
Chambersburg PA
CBHW040817120726
48005CB00012B/1442